Pearls Blows Up

Other *Pearls Before Swine* Collections

When Pigs Fly

50,000,000 Pearls Fans Can't Be Wrong

The Saturday Evening Pearls

Macho Macho Animals

The Sopratos

Da Brudderhood of Zeeba Zeeba Eata

The Ratvolution Will Not Be Televised

Nighthogs

This Little Piggy Stayed Home

BLTs Taste So Darn Good

Treasuries

Pearls Sells Out

The Crass Menagerie

Lions and Tigers and Crocs, Oh My!

Sgt. Piggy's Lonely Hearts Club Comic

Gift Book

Da Crockydile Book o' Frendsheep

Pearls Blows Up

A *Pearls Before Swine* Treasury

by Stephan Pastis

**Andrews McMeel
Publishing, LLC**

Kansas City • Sydney • London

Pearls Before Swine is distributed internationally by United Feature Syndicate.

Pearls Blows Up copyright © 2011 by Stephan Pastis. All rights reserved. Printed in the United States of America. No part of this book may be used or reproduced in any manner whatsoever without written permission except in the case of reprints in the context of reviews.

Andrews McMeel Publishing, LLC
an Andrews McMeel Universal company
1130 Walnut Street, Kansas City, Missouri 64106

www.andrewsmcmeel.com

11 12 13 14 15 BAM 10 9 8 7 6 5 4 3 2 1

ISBN: 978-1-4494-0106-1

Library of Congress Control Number: 2010930547

Pearls Before Swine can be viewed on the Internet at
www.pearlscomic.com

These strips appeared in newspapers from February 17, 2008, to August 22, 2009.

For my dad, Tom Pastis, who wins every time we play pool, unless I cheat, which is fairly common.

Introduction

I've never watched a single episode of *Star Trek*. I've never seen a movie about a superhero. And I don't read comic books.

In short, if you were to design my personal Hell, it would look a lot like a comic convention.

Which is where I went in the summer of 2009.

The event was Comic-Con in San Diego. It's the biggest convention of its kind, and they asked me to be a guest. All I had to do was give a presentation and sign books afterwards.

I should add here that I'm not big on book signings either.

Weird things happen at book signings. I'll list a few of the dependable ones:

• At least one person always hands me a music CD of the band they're in, as though I'm a record label executive and can get them signed.

• Some bizarre fan always stands right next to me and won't leave my side, often following me until I get back into my car and lock the door, hopefully with him on the outside.

• One fan will always ask me to write something very specific in a book they're buying for their friend, and it is almost always something very insulting about that friend and/or the friend's alma mater, such as "To Bob, You Really Suck and So Do the Duke Blue Devils. F#@$ You."

Then there is the *random* weirdness.

Like the guy who ran up to me the moment I was done speaking to accuse me of ripping off an episode of his friend's Web comic that appeared eight years ago.

Or the guy who slammed a cap with his company's logo on my head and quickly had a friend snap a picture, as though I was endorsing the company.

Or the woman who told me all was fine in her life until the CIA started following her (she also handed me a CD of her husband's band, so she was a double winner in my book).

Given my dislike of comic conventions and book signings, saying no to Comic-Con should have been easy, but it was not, because it entailed two things I absolutely cannot resist; two things that have the power to defeat the badness of comic conventions:

• Sitting by the pool;

• Drinking.

Comic-Con meant four days of this at a great hotel in the beautiful city of San Diego, all free (well, not the alcohol, technically, but there are ways of making a bar receipt look like a lunch receipt, and I may have taken advantage of that).

I brought my wife, Staci, with me the first day, thinking she would enjoy sitting by the pool as much as me. But in a stunning error of judgment, she decided we had to walk the convention floor.

And just like that, I was in a land not even Dante could have envisioned.

People dressed like animals. People dressed like superheroes. People dressed like *Star Wars* characters.

And they don't just dress like them, they *act* like them.

Take my word on this. There is nothing more disturbing in all of human existence than watching a forty-five-year-old man dressed like a Stormtrooper battle a fifty-two-year-old man dressed like Luke Skywalker.

It is the kind of debauchery that made God flood the earth in the time of Noah and surely must tempt him to do it again.

So I ran from the convention and didn't look back, afraid that if I did, I would turn into a pillar of salt.

And for the next four days I sat by the pool at the Marriott and drank cold drinks, all day, every day (okay, fine, I ran over there to do my speech and sign books, but believe me, I sprinted back).

And those four days were the funnest four days of the summer.

They were made even more fun because after Staci left, I invited my friend Emilio to come down to San Diego. Emilio shares all of my drinking and tanning priorities and had absolutely no desire to attend the convention itself or even get near the people who did. (In fact, it was everything I could do to keep him from leaving the hotel after he encountered two guys dressed like Iron Man arguing in the hotel elevator over whose costume was more authentic.)

The whole trip was such a success that I soon began to think I could do this in one sunny city after another.

So right after I got home, I went online and found a really great comic convention in a city I love (but probably shouldn't name), complete with great beaches and a whole bunch of great bars, and e-mailed the guy who ran it.

He wrote back within a half hour and said sure, he'd love to have me as a guest.

Shazam.

I had done it.

All I had to do now was call Emilio and remind him to bring the bottle opener.

That's when I did some more research. Research I probably should have done *before* e-mailing the guy who ran the convention.

And found out this:

The convention site was an hour away from the beach and all of the good bars. It wasn't really *in* the city I loved. It was just sort of *near* it. All by itself. In the middle of nowhere.

I called the convention guy.

"Hi there," I said, "I'm the guy who e-mailed you, and I was just wondering if I can ask you a few questions."

"Sure," he said.

"I was looking online, and it looks like the hotel is all by itself, sort of far away from the beach and the bars."

"Oh, yeah," he said. "Those are about forty-five minutes away, unless there's traffic; then it takes even longer."

"Hmmm," I said. "So what do guests do?"

"What do you mean, 'What do guests do?' They attend the convention."

"Oh, sure," I said, "but what about after? Like when they want to go to the downtown bars?"

"Why would they do that? Everything they want is right here."

That confused me.

"You mean like a pool and bars and stuff?" I asked.

"Cartoonists to meet. Panels to attend. Places to get signed books. Meet other fans."

Now I was dumbfounded.

"So there's no pool?" I asked.

"No," he said.

"And no bars?"

"No," he said, losing patience.

There was silence on both ends of the phone.

"Listen," he offered, "You don't have to decide now, but just so you know, we're gonna have a large turnout because we have some big names coming. TV actors."

Uninterested though I was, I had to ask.

"Who?" I said.

He paused and lowered his voice for effect.

"You ever watch *Star Trek*?"

–Stephan Pastis
March 2011

There is a good way to draw water and a bad way. This is a worse way. What a crappy opening to an otherwise fine book.

There is one particular newspaper chain (I won't say which one) that does not like it when I reference the declining fortunes of newspapers, even when it's just a throwaway line such as in the last panel here. Now when I do it, they remove that particular strip from that day's paper and run a replacement strip instead.

I am not very generous when it comes to giving gifts. Although I have yet to give used hotel soap.

Look at all the effort that went into drawing the headstones in that second panel. I say the second, and not the third, because the ones in the third are all cut-and-pasted. God bless you, Photoshop.

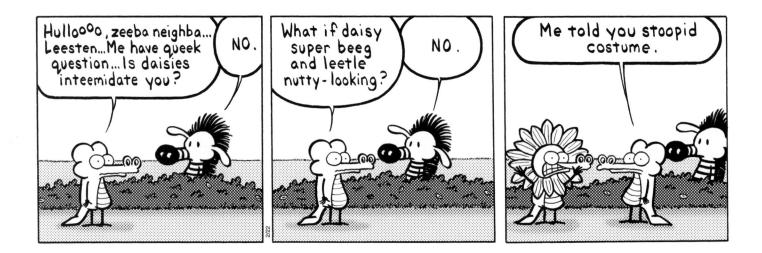

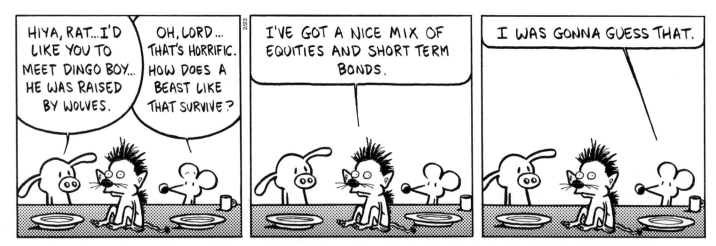

Whenever one of the characters says, "Oh, God" or "Oh, Lord," I always get at least one complaint about using the Lord's name in vain.

Speaking of garages, I backed my car into our garage door last year. It did a lot of damage. So here's a safety tip: Open your garage door before you back your car out.

I should have given him a beer instead of wine. There's no way hyenas are wine drinkers.

The way you know that's an antelope and not Goat is by looking at the dialogue bubble where the hyena calls him an antelope.

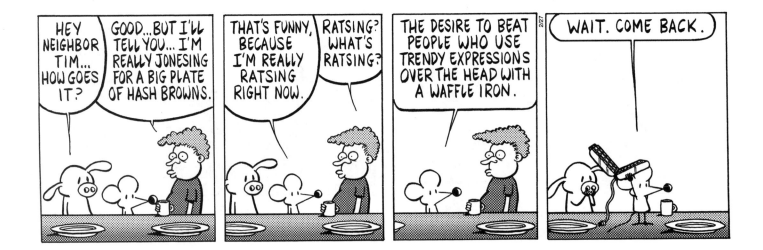

This was a funny strip when it was in my head. Then it got put onto paper.

This breaks a cardinal rule in *Pearls*: Never draw anything with wheels. Why? Because it comes out looking like this thing.

I have to admit that when I am stuck at the doctor's or dentist's office, I seek out the *People* magazine. But I hide the cover so no one can see what I'm reading.

This series came about as a result of a concierge who e-mailed me with the various complaints he had about his job. I just took each of the situations he mentioned and gave them to Rat to handle.

The concierge who e-mailed me told me that this was his biggest pet peeve. People constantly asked him for restaurant recommendations, and after he'd give them one, they'd reply, "Is it good?" As though he didn't understand the concept of restaurant recommendations.

I think I had the Springsteen song "It's Hard to Be a Saint in the City" in my mind when I wrote the line in the last panel.

Because all of these complaints came from an actual concierge, the strips resonated with a number of people in the profession, many of whom wanted to know if I had ever been a concierge.

I think this was the one and only time I ever drew a female lion in the strip.

One of the unspoken rules of comics is that you can always indicate the female sex of an otherwise gender-neutral-looking animal by putting a bow on her head. But do any girls still wear bows on their heads? It seems to me that the only thing all girls now have in common is a tattoo on their lower back. Maybe I'll make that the new comic strip shorthand for girls.

Look at that unique camera angle in Panel 2. I am the Martin Scorsese of the comics page but without the fame, money, or talent.

I was a bit worried about this strip because it mentioned Jesus. That's guaranteed to bunch up the panties of a few sensitive folk. In fact, using the expression "bunch up the panties" could also bunch up the panties of a few sensitive folk.

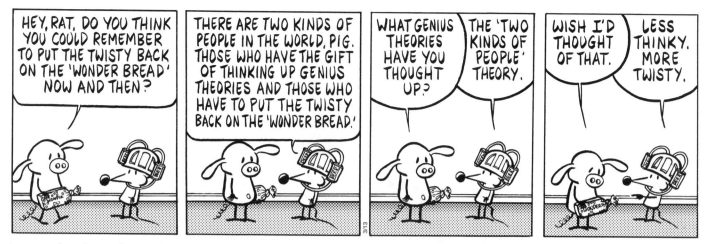

I am in the class of people that does not put the twisty back on. I do, however, spin the bread package closed and squish the spinny end against the refrigerator wall, in the hopes that it will stay closed.

My wife and I recently bought a condo so I could have a place where I can draw the strip. The best part about it is that I do not know any of my neighbors. I haven't even met them. Sometimes that involves going to great lengths. For example, when I'm outside and I see their garage door opening, I run inside.

When I wrestle with my kids, I always let them beat me initially. Then, when I'm pinned to the ground, I hum the *Popeye* theme and pour an imaginary can of spinach in my mouth. That's when they run.

I'm always tempted to make *Ratimus Studimus Maximus* the title of a book collection.

As a kid, I would try to turn the spoon really rapidly, to see if I could somehow catch the spoon napping and thereby see my reflection right-side-up. But it never worked. I was always upside-down. When I say I did this "as a kid," I mean last week.

My strip has a lot of cardboard boxes. That's my contribution to the field of cartooning.

I'm Greek Orthodox, so we have a different Easter than everyone else. So after every Easter, when people ask me how my holiday was, I always have to say, "I haven't had my Easter yet." Then they stare at me like I'm a freak. Which I am. But for different reasons.

Now I've got guys carrying boxes while standing in boxes. This is out of control.

This was my favorite one of the Eet-a-Zeeb strips.

Mentioning gypsies always triggers letters from people who say it's somehow racist. So I made sure to include the father from *Baby Blues* here in the hopes that I would confuse any would-be complainers into thinking they were reading a *Baby Blues* strip.

It's always hard when your first contact with another cartoonist is to say, "Hi, I'm Stephan Pastis, and I'm having one of your main characters search for a female escort in my comic." But that's what happened when I called *Sally Forth* creator Francesco ("Ces") Marciuliano and told him what I was doing with his character Ted Forth. I then took it a step further and asked if there was any way that in his strip, he could put Ted in a hotel on the day my strip ran. That way, *Sally Forth* readers would see Ted Forth in a hotel lobby, and when they read *Pearls*, they would see what illicit things Ted was actually trying to do in that hotel lobby. Not only did Ces do it, but he actually had Ted talking to the hotel concierge that day, making the crossover all the more obvious. Readers who saw both strips really seemed to like it.

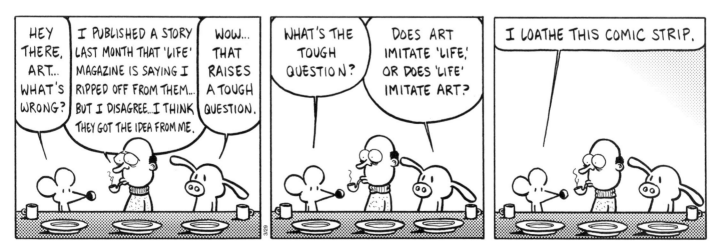

Danny Donkey was sad.

Sad because everyone around him was good-looking. And he was not.

So Danny Donkey went to a genie and asked to be good-looking.

"That is too much work on my part," said the genie, "But I can give you this."

And with that, the genie handed over what appeared to be some magical rod, and told Danny what it was and how to use it.

And so, later that day, Danny went out and hit every good-looking person he could find with his very own Ugly Stick.

KONK

"BECAUSE, KIDS, IF YOU CAN'T MAKE YOURSELF BETTER, MAKE THOSE AROUND YOU WORSE."

THIS IS **NOT** GOING IN A CHILDREN'S BOOK.

HEY... MAYBE I GOT HIT BY THAT THING.

Looking back on this strip, I'm wondering why I had all the good-looking people wear identical clothes. It's sad when your own strip perplexes you.

28

This was a really popular strip.

I really liked this strip, as well as the next two that followed. But after I drew them, I showed them to my son Tom, and he didn't laugh. That concerned me because Tom is such a good barometer for the strip. Sure enough, when the strips ran, they got a lukewarm reaction.

The real Green Zone is the American-controlled area in Baghdad, Iraq. Little did I know that eighteen months after this strip ran, I would actually be in the Green Zone on a USO-sponsored trip to Iraq.

For such a weak joke, I went to an awful lot of trouble drawing that couch.

I liked the way this strip turned out. That's one of the mysteries of doing comic strips. All the ideas seem decent when you come up with them, but when you actually draw the strip, some turn out better than you thought they would and some turn out worse. And unfortunately, you don't really know until it's too late to do anything about it.

That's supposed to be Saddam Hussein in the last panel. But the only way for a reader to know that is to wait a couple years after the strip runs and read the commentary in this treasury book.

I tried to imitate random Arabic letters on that TV screen, but after I did it, I got kind of scared wondering if I had actually spelled a real word that could somehow be offensive. So I had my editor at United check with someone who could read Arabic. He assured us I had not spelled a real word.

There's no way Larry's body could realistically fit into that KFC bucket, even allowing for the generous rules of cartoon physics. Even sadder is how I didn't discover this error until today, when I was doing the commentary for this book.

That's supposed to be Osama bin Laden in the last panel. Sadly, he's about as recognizable as Saddam Hussein was a few days earlier. That brings up an important rule of cartooning: If the joke is dependent on the reader recognizing someone in the last panel, it's a good idea to make that person recognizable.

I think my strip rivals *Andy Capp* for beer consumption. I'm proud of that.

And just like that I merge the concierge storyline with the Eet-a-Zeeb storyline. I am one creative fellow.

I think I was inspired here by Homer Simpson's famous line, "Save me, Jeebus!!" When I say "inspired," I mean I stole the idea from someone else.

I liked this joke. But now I'm wondering why I went to the trouble of drawing those poorly drawn buildings in the window.

Have you ever wandered out of your hotel room in just your boxers to get some ice from the ice machine two doors down, only to have your hotel door close behind you? And of course you didn't bring your hotel key, so you have to go down the elevator in your boxers to get a new key from the front desk, and the whole time down the elevator you're trying to build up your courage by saying to yourself over and over, "Boxers look just like swim trunks. Boxers look just like swim trunks." I've done that.

This was my little tribute to *Family Guy* following my visit to their offices in 2007. The best part was the *Family Guy* pinball machine in the lobby. That's a great pinball machine.

Take a close look at the cover of Pig's magazine in the first panel. It's a reference to Mark Tatulli's pantomime character, Liō. The headline reads, "Liō kid waterboarded. Won't talk." The magazine cover changes in the second and third panels, where it says, "All Comic Strips Now in Repeats" and "Comic Strip Polls the Answer to Everything."

I seem to draw a lot of bald men. Boxes and bald men. Those are my contributions to cartooning.

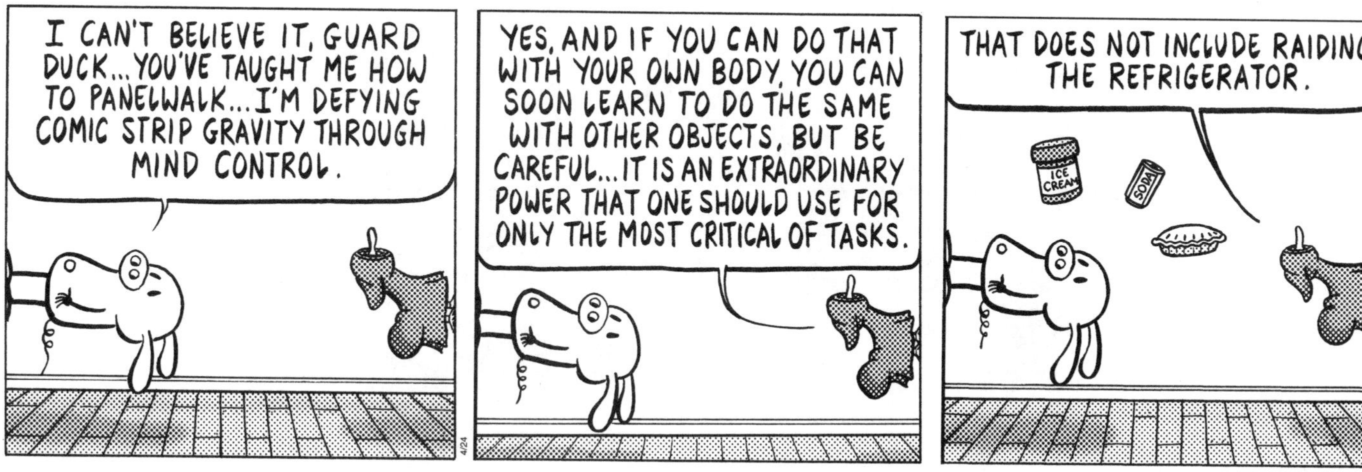
I CAN'T BELIEVE IT, GUARD DUCK... YOU'VE TAUGHT ME HOW TO PANELWALK... I'M DEFYING COMIC STRIP GRAVITY THROUGH MIND CONTROL.
YES, AND IF YOU CAN DO THAT WITH YOUR OWN BODY, YOU CAN SOON LEARN TO DO THE SAME WITH OTHER OBJECTS, BUT BE CAREFUL... IT IS AN EXTRAORDINARY POWER THAT ONE SHOULD USE FOR ONLY THE MOST CRITICAL OF TASKS.
THAT DOES NOT INCLUDE RAIDING THE REFRIGERATOR.
ICE CREAM
SODA

Look at that pie. You can almost tell it's a pie.

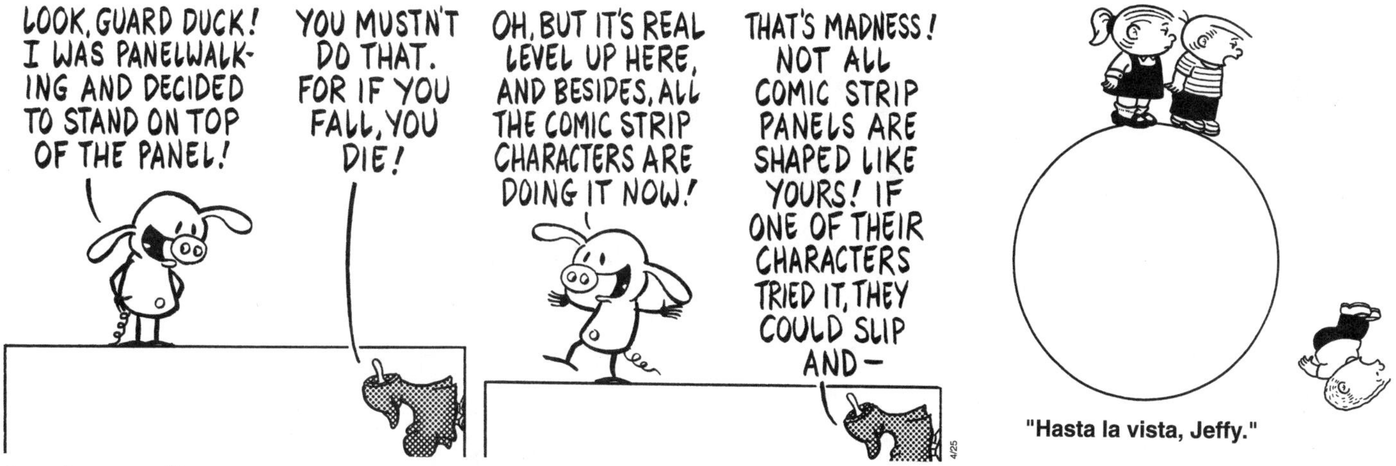
LOOK, GUARD DUCK! I WAS PANELWALKING AND DECIDED TO STAND ON TOP OF THE PANEL!
YOU MUSTN'T DO THAT. FOR IF YOU FALL, YOU DIE!
OH, BUT IT'S REAL LEVEL UP HERE, AND BESIDES, ALL THE COMIC STRIP CHARACTERS ARE DOING IT NOW!
THAT'S MADNESS! NOT ALL COMIC STRIP PANELS ARE SHAPED LIKE YOURS! IF ONE OF THEIR CHARACTERS TRIED IT, THEY COULD SLIP AND—
"Hasta la vista, Jeffy."

I've drawn Jeffy so many times I'm starting to think he may be one of *my* characters. I should sue the Keanes for copyright infringement.

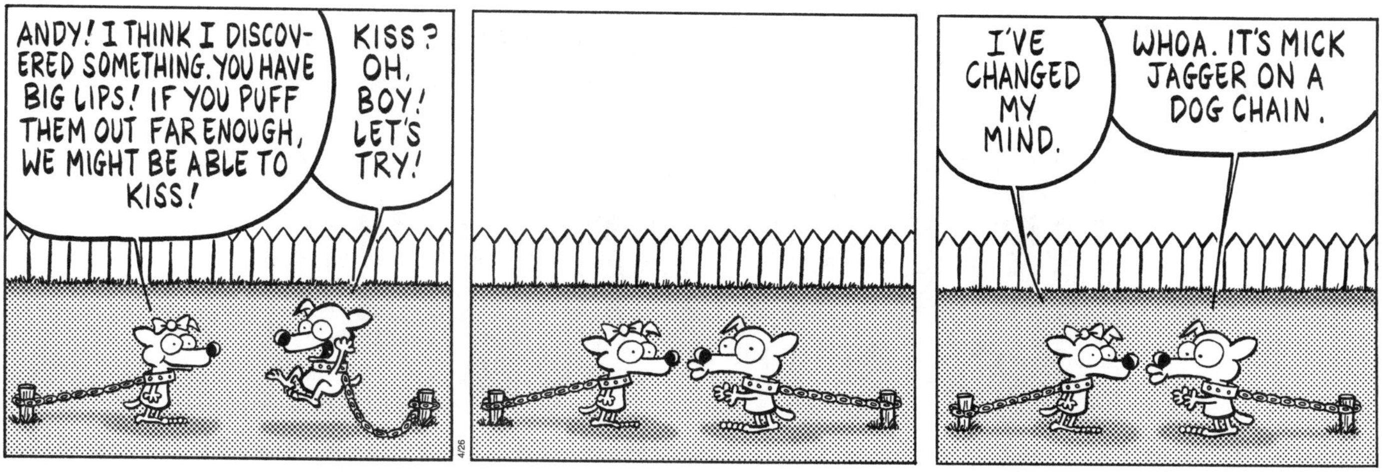
ANDY! I THINK I DISCOVERED SOMETHING. YOU HAVE BIG LIPS! IF YOU PUFF THEM OUT FAR ENOUGH, WE MIGHT BE ABLE TO KISS!
KISS? OH, BOY! LET'S TRY!
I'VE CHANGED MY MIND.
WHOA. IT'S MICK JAGGER ON A DOG CHAIN.

Some people didn't get this because they didn't know Mick Jagger is known for having big lips. For those same people I should probably go ahead and mention that Mick Jagger is in a rock-and-roll band called the Rolling Stones. They are moderately successful.

For those people who had always complained up to this point that Andy was a sad character, I kept thinking to myself, "You think that's sad? Wait 'til you see what happens with his girlfriend. Now *that's* sad." I guess I figured that if the Andy character was going to depress them, I might as well *really* depress them.

This was a very popular image of Pig. In fact, one reader sent me a photo showing that she had it tattooed on her arm.

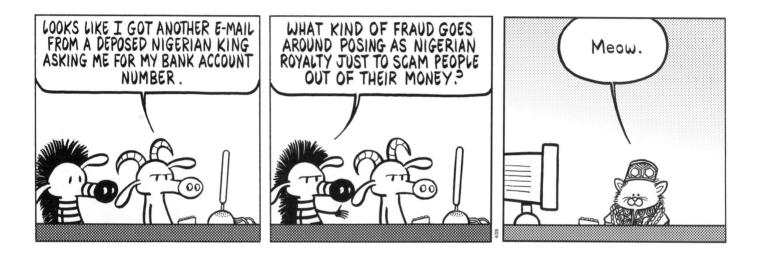

For this strip, I walked from my drawing room to our dining room and tried to draw our chandelier. Then I realized I was standing in my boxers right in front of the living room windows. And now I just realized this is the second time in just a few pages that I've told a story involving me and my boxers.

My grandfather loved figs. And that, my friends, is the kind of inside knowledge you paid extra for when you bought this treasury.

I call this kind of strip structure an "inside cut-away." A cut-away panel is one where you shift up the scene (cut from one locale to a different locale). I normally do the cut-aways in the last panel. But this one's right in the middle of the strip. Moreover, I think it makes me look really smart to make up my own terms and then explain them to you.

I was lucky enough to recently write an animated special for *Peanuts*. You'll be glad to know that I never had Charlie Brown yell, "Holy $#*@!!"

This was a fun joke in my head. Then I had to draw all those Rice Krispies guys, and it got less fun.

I never got to eat Trix as a kid. My mom made me eat healthy cereal she bought from some health food store. It had no sugar. I made up for it by dumping four spoonfuls of sugar on each bowl of cereal, thereby negating the entire reason for buying cereal from the health food store.

That is one well-drawn newspaper rack. It even has the little "$.50" printed by the coin slot. Some days I am really, really talented.

Wow, that's not a badly drawn monkey. I am on an artistic roll.

Uh oh. A truck. My drawing streak ends at two. It was fun while it lasted.

I think there was some symbolism to the items the happy guy was jumping on in that second row of panels. But now I can't remember what it was. Oh well, go ahead and make it up for yourselves.

Little did I know that by the end of the year, I would be doing my own blog (www.stephanpastis.wordpress.com).

The most popular strip of the year. And it came from real life. I was walking through an aquarium in San Francisco with my daughter. She pointed to a moray eel and asked me what it was. When I said, "That's a moray," the woman next to us laughed. So I thought it would make a good strip.

I must have had the paper at a strange angle when I drew this, because Pig is angled way too much to the right in the first and third panels.

This was a much more popular strip than I thought it would be. I think it was just because so many people hate algebra.

I see I found a new feature on Photoshop.

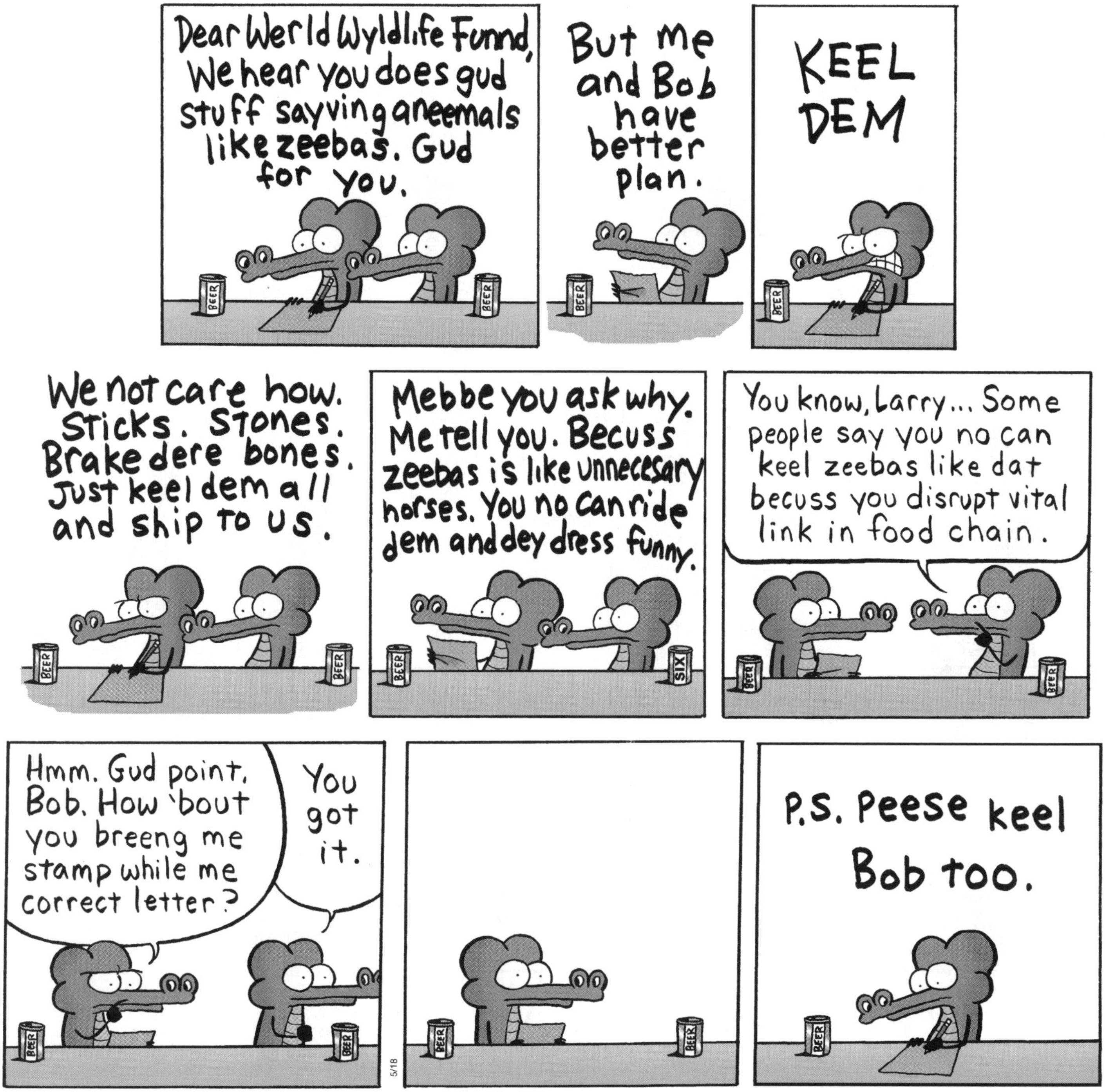
Dear Werld Wyldlife Funnd, We hear you does gud stuff sayving aneemals like zeebas. Gud for you.
BEER
BEER
But me and Bob have better plan.
BEER
KEEL DEM
BEER
We not care how. Sticks. Stones. Brake dere bones. Just keel dem all and ship to us.
BEER
BEER
Mebbe you ask why. Me tell you. Becuss zeebas is like unnecesary horses. You no can ride dem and dey dress funny.
BEER
SIX
You know, Larry... Some people say you no can keel zeebas like dat becuss you disrupt vital link in food chain.
BEER
BEER
Hmm. Gud point, Bob. How 'bout you breeng me stamp while me correct letter?
You got it.
BEER
BEER
5/18
BEER
BEER
P.S. Peese keel Bob too.
BEER

Somebody told me that after seeing this strip, they actually tried doing this with their cable bill. No word on how the cable company responded.

Odd that they're washing so many socks in a family where nobody wears them.

How come everybody complains when I put the little dog Andy on a chain, but nobody says a word when I put a cat in a cage? That's unfair to cats. Maybe I'll send a complaint to myself.

I just want to say how proud I am that I snuck the word "doobie" into a newspaper comic strip.

51

I'm hoping that somebody out there really tries to make this diorama. It would be one heckuva diorama.

Strips that make fun of stupid people are almost guaranteed to be popular. I guess everyone feels besieged by stupid people.

George W. Bush obviously had an effect on Rat.

Can I just tell you how long it took me to draw that Jack? I should have chosen an Ace.

The Jack's line in the last panel triggered a bit of a debate with my syndicate over whether the correct term is "Homes" or "Holmes." I thought it was "Holmes," as in "Sherlock Holmes," because you say it to people when what they're saying is painfully obvious and thus you're sarcastically referring to them as "Sherlock Holmes." My syndicate told me it was "Homes," as in "Homey." Shows what I know.

First time I've ever had a character talk from two different places on his body.

I think this is one of my favorite *Pearls* strips, mostly because I think there's a lot of truth to it. By the way, only the most pitiful cartoonists praise their own work like that.

More Andy. More complaints. At least his girlfriend isn't leaving him in this one.

For those who don't know, the last panel is a reference to Gene Kelly in *Singin' in the Rain*. I've never seen it.

I didn't really love this strip, so I ran it on a Saturday, as I do all my strips that I don't like.

That's me under the "Stupido" category in Panel 2. (And me saying, "I draw a comic strip" in Panel 4.)

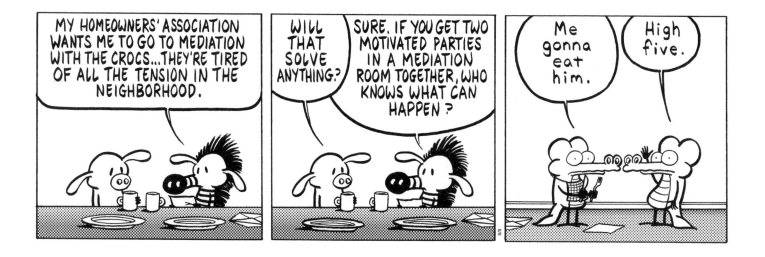

As a lawyer, I used to go to a lot of these mediations. My characterization of them is not far off.

Not one Venezuelan complained about this strip. That may be due to the fact that not one Venezuelan read this strip.

I like the croc pose in the third panel. It's how my friends and I mock each other.

Now that I look at it, I see that I sort of assumed everyone would know basic Spanish, which of course they don't. So I should say here that the translation of that last line is, "Where is Hugo Chávez?" If that didn't make you laugh, feel free to come up with your own translation.

This strip received a huge reaction, all of it positive. Well, almost all of it. One woman wrote to accuse me of tarnishing the reputation of Martin Luther King, Jr. But she was humorless, so I won't count her.

After my experience with Turkey (see the last treasury), I half expected a complaint letter from the Venezuelan embassy about this series. Fortunately, I did not get one. Unlike Turkey, they apparently have more important things to do.

This strip was very popular. (Now that I think about it, how do you know that's true? I could just be making it up and saying it after any strip I want to.)

This strip was very popular.

This strip was very popular.

This strip was very popular.

One day while driving home from the café where I sometimes write the strip, I actually ran over a squirrel. While most people would say to themselves, "Ahhh, I feel terrible," I said to myself, "A strip idea!"

I bought a Bluetooth once, but I felt really stupid walking around with it in my ear, so I returned it the next day.

Something's off about this strip. I think it's Zebra's line in the last panel. It's too cliché or something. Not that that normally stops me, but here it just reads clunky. So if you have a thick Sharpie with you, go ahead and cross this strip out of the book.

This strip triggered a really angry e-mail from a travel agent, who complained that I had tarnished her entire profession. Now that I think about it, maybe she was the same woman who wrote me about Martin Luther King.

If I were mayor of a town, my first act in office would be to make whistling a misdemeanor. No human being should ever whistle in the presence of another.

This really would work. I'm gonna try it the next time a friend e-mails me asking for a favor.

All I remember about this strip is that my friend Eric told me he liked it. Eric is the executive producer of a great show on MTV called *Bully Beatdown*, where school bullies get beaten up by mixed martial arts fighters. I'm always tempted to do a week of strips where Rat goes on the show and gets beaten up by some mammoth MMA fighter.

I HEAR YOU GOT A JOB WRITING EPITAPHS.

YES, BUT IT'S HARD TO SUM UP A PERSON'S LIFE RESPECTFULLY IN JUST A FEW LINES. HERE, LOOK AT ONE I JUST DID....

Here layeth Bob. Who never got a job. But don't be sad, be sunny. He's done leeching your money.

I DON'T THINK I'LL HIRE YOU.

HEY... DOES ANYTHING RHYME WITH "DRUNKEN HOBO"?

HEY, RAT... WHAT ARE YOU DOING?

WELL, SINCE I GOT A JOB WRITING EPITAPHS, I THOUGHT I'D WRITE YOURS.

DO I WANT TO SEE THIS?

OH, SURE.. IT'S MORE COMPLIMENTARY THAN YOU'D PROBABLY IMAGINE.

He drew cartoons, but they were rotten. And that is why He's now forgotten.

YOU SEEM UPSET.

The greatest epitaphs are on the graves on Boot Hill in Tombstone, Arizona. One of them says, "Here lies Lester Moore. Four slugs from a .44. No Les, no more."

WHATSA MATTER WITH YOU?

MY BACK HURT, SO MY DOCTOR GAVE ME PAIN KILLERS. BUT I THINK I TOOK TOO MUCH. I FEEL WEIRD.

HOW DO YOU MEAN WEIRD?

WEIRD.

HOW WEIRD?

I GOTTA GO.

When I look back on this strip, I think it was *me* who must have been on painkillers. It's just so odd.

My little homage to Abbott and Costello's "Who's on First?" routine.

One syndicated cartoonist (who shall go unnamed) thought this was an unnecessarily rude shot at *For Better or For Worse* creator Lynn Johnston and told me all about it in a rather abrupt e-mail. I felt like writing back, "Hey, if you thought today's strip was rude, wait 'til you see tomorrow's."

I never heard back from that same cartoonist about this particular strip. I guess that among cartoonists, *Family Circus* is fair game, even if that involves reptiles eating one of the kids.

While I wasn't the first syndicated cartoonist to draw himself in a strip, I wanted to be the first to kill himself in a strip. Hence my own death. Come to think of it, what if I had actually died on the day this strip had ran? That would have been something.

Rat and I are a bit too intimate in this pose.

In the strip *Funky Winkerbean*, its creator Tom Batiuk had a long, very touching storyline where one of his characters died of cancer. In the strip where she died, she met this particular fellow in heaven. I asked Tom if I could literally cut and paste the character into my own strip so that he could meet Rat and me when we died. Being the good sport that he is, he agreed.

Predictably, this strip was posted on a lot of people's blogs.

This final image is one of the images on the 2010 *Pearls* wall calendar. Note how subtly I slipped in that plug.

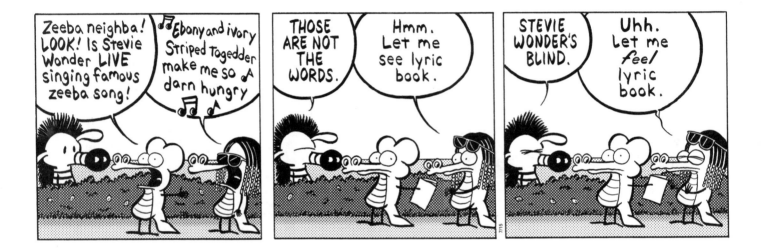

I have to admit that when I was a kid, *Happy Days* was by far my favorite TV show.

I think I resorted to this formula one too many times. By that I mean the type of strip where the characters talk about somebody doing something shady, and then I cut away to the cat. But I have to say that when you do a strip, and you're responsible for 365 new ideas a year, it's hard to resist the lure of doing something you know has worked in the past. Of course, at some point you're at risk of making the strip formulaic. And I think that's what happened here.

Ironically, I now have a Facebook page that I update with character art, news, and other info, like how to get signed books. Here is the link: http://www.facebook.com/pages/Stephan-Pastis/132583843763?ref=ts. Sadly, this plug isn't nearly as subtle as the last one.

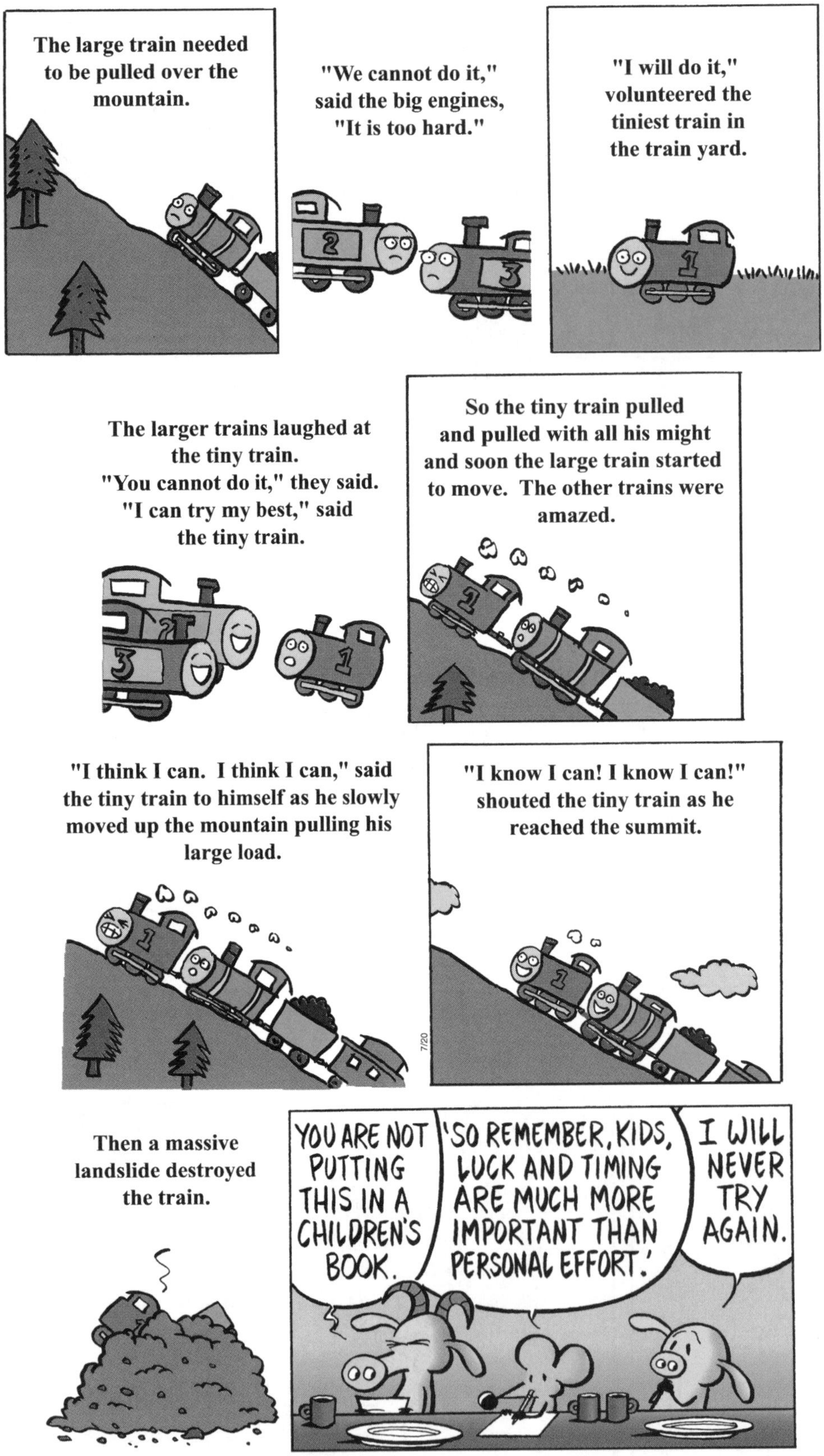
The large train needed to be pulled over the mountain.
"We cannot do it," said the big engines, "It is too hard."
"I will do it," volunteered the tiniest train in the train yard.
The larger trains laughed at the tiny train. "You cannot do it," they said. "I can try my best," said the tiny train.
So the tiny train pulled and pulled with all his might and soon the large train started to move. The other trains were amazed.
"I think I can. I think I can," said the tiny train to himself as he slowly moved up the mountain pulling his large load.
"I know I can! I know I can!" shouted the tiny train as he reached the summit.
Then a massive landslide destroyed the train.
YOU ARE NOT PUTTING THIS IN A CHILDREN'S BOOK.
'SO REMEMBER, KIDS, LUCK AND TIMING ARE MUCH MORE IMPORTANT THAN PERSONAL EFFORT.'
I WILL NEVER TRY AGAIN.

Fart jokes are a sure way to get complaints from newspaper readers. But here, my use of the word "toots" got none. Maybe some people thought Pig's girlfriend was blowing a horn.

I don't know what these hats are called, but I call them *Fargo* hats, because the lead character in that movie wears one. Something about them just strikes me as funny.

At the risk of looking like a tool, I must say that I liked the line, "When you reach for the stars, you catch a handful of critics." Speaking of which, a comics historian recently called me an "insult to cartooning." I think I'll put that on one of my book covers.

Alright, this one took me by complete surprise. I just thought it was a weak strip, so I tucked it on a Saturday. But after it appeared, I got a number of angry e-mails from people saying they knew a twin who had died, and this wasn't funny in the least. And their e-mails were filled with so much anger you'd think they were blaming *me* for their death. So let me just say here: No twins were harmed in the making of this comic strip.

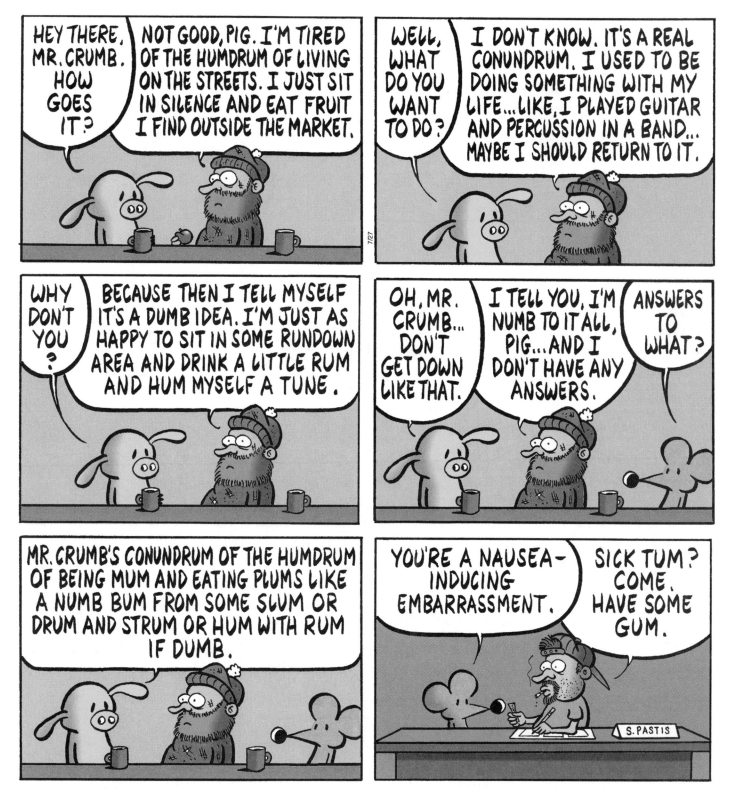

This strip took me forever to write, but it wasn't nearly as popular as I thought it would be. That hurt my feelings. In time, I'm hoping to recover my self-esteem.

I wonder the same thing when I'm in coffee shops. Of course, I don't really have a job either.

Why do they put missing people on milk cartons? Why don't they put them on beer? Wouldn't people who drink beer be more likely to have criminal tips than people who drink milk? You know, I'm pretty smart for a cartoonist.

I call my mom and dad every week. My sisters do not. I'm hoping that my mom and dad remember that when they write their wills.

The premise for this strip makes no sense. Hold your hand over the strip and turn the page.

I think I saw Darby Conley have one of his characters reach out and over the panel line in *Get Fuzzy*. So I did it with the croc in the fifth panel of this strip. Some people would call that a copyright infringement. I call it an "homage."

That's my pet name for my wife, Staci.

On the off chance that Staci might actually read this book, I'm gonna go ahead now and apologize for that last comment.

People occasionally write me to express their disgust at Pig's taste for pig-based products. But he's been that way since the very beginning of the strip. In fact, for those who've never seen it, the first *Pearls* book has Pig on the cover eating a sandwich, and the title is *BLTs Taste So Darn Good*.

I can't stand change. For example, I sleep in these comfortable sweatpants I call Magipants, which is short for "Magic Pants." Staci recently tried to buy me a second pair of sleeping pants. They were nothing like the original Magipants. In fact, they were an insult to Magipants. It really upset me.

If I haven't said it before, let me say it here: Soccer balls are ridiculously hard to draw. The pattern involves one pentagon surrounded by five hexagons. If any one of the shapes is off, the whole pattern is off. So from now on, Andy will only be playing with baseballs and basketballs.

I thought Pig came out cute here.

As much as I liked the last Pig drawing, I hated this one. I drew it five or six times and could never get it right. So if you still have that black Sharpie you used to cross out prior strips, use it here to draw your own third panel.

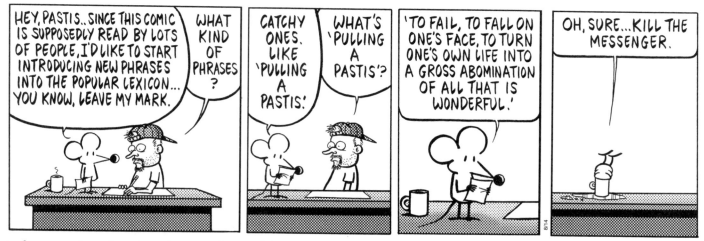

I often wonder what the other members of the Pastis clan think about strips such as this.

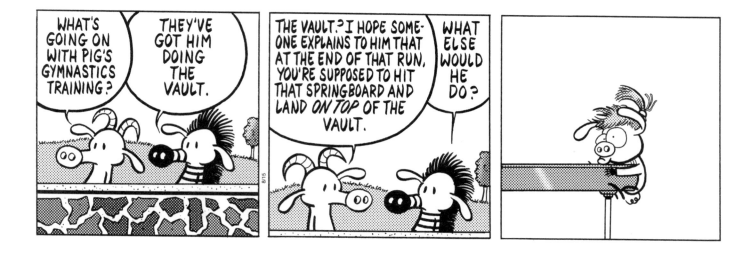

This doesn't really work because you don't know that the pause in Panel 2 is supposed to be momentary (in other words, Rat gives meditation only a fleeting second to work). This might work better in animation.

Holy smokes, I've drawn myself like a fat, swarthy troll in this one.

Rat is supposed to look like Ernest Hemingway here. I'm a big Hemingway fan.

I often wonder if some friends and relatives are afraid of doing stupid things around me for fear that it will end up in the strip. It does.

This happens with ideas I write down in the middle of the night. In my semi-asleep state, they sound brilliant. In the morning, they sound incomprehensible.

My tribute to George Herriman's comic, *Krazy Kat*. I ran it on what would have been Herriman's 128th birthday.

Since this strip depends on the reader filling in profanity in the fifth panel, I was a little worried about it. Sounds stupid, but dumb stuff like this can really get you into trouble in the Sunday comics. So I ran the strip in late August, figuring that most people were on vacation and not reading the comics.

To be honest with you, I wasn't sure that's what storm drains do, so I had to Google it. I lead a sad, sheltered life.

For some strange reason, it looks like I used a ruler to draw that rain. That is some bad rain.

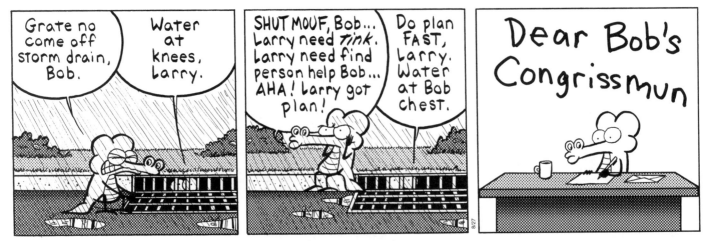

No more ruler. Much better rain. Darn it, I *learn* from my mistakes.

I've always had this vague fear that snakes could come up through my toilet and bite me while I'm doing No. 2. That would be a bad experience for the both of us.

Since I've already confessed this much, I might as well go ahead and say I love to read in the bathroom. During each visit, I try to cover at least ten pages of whatever book I'm reading. Unless a snake bites me in the you-know-what.

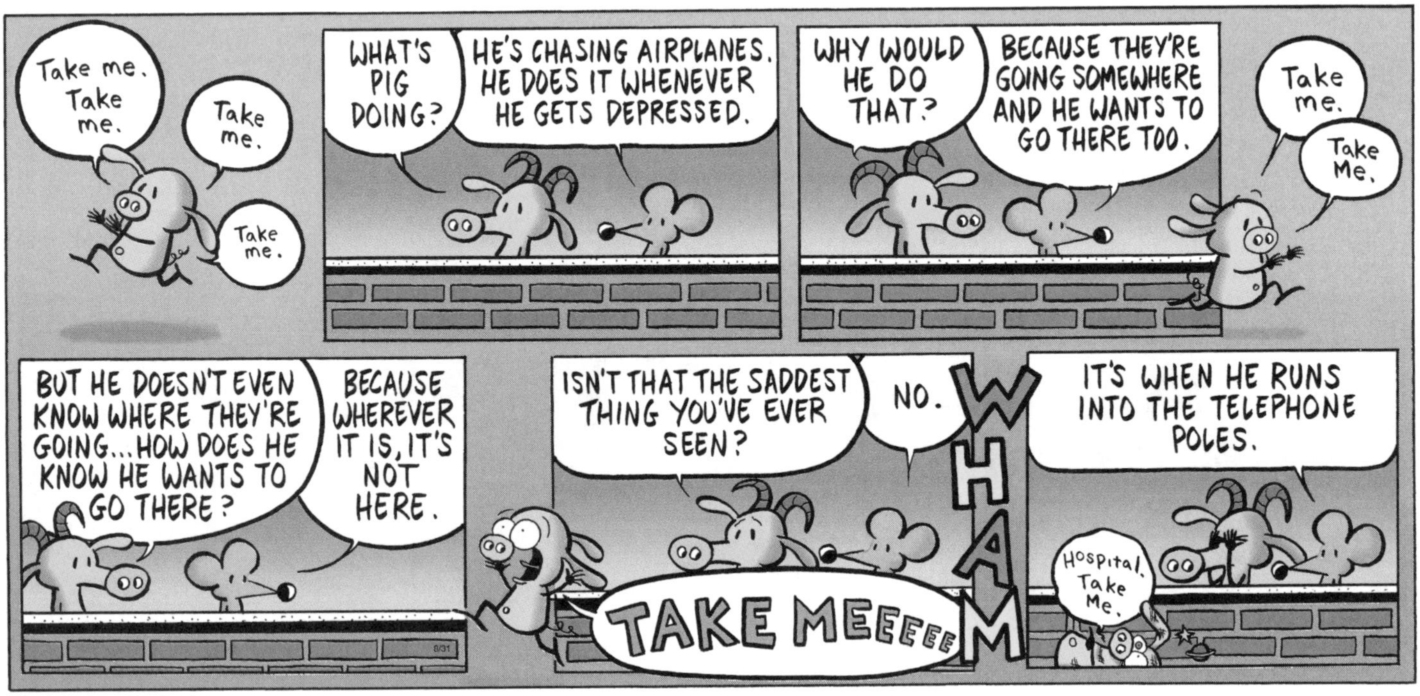
Take me. Take me.
Take me.
Take me.
WHAT'S PIG DOING?
HE'S CHASING AIRPLANES. HE DOES IT WHENEVER HE GETS DEPRESSED.
WHY WOULD HE DO THAT?
BECAUSE THEY'RE GOING SOMEWHERE AND HE WANTS TO GO THERE TOO.
Take me.
Take Me.
BUT HE DOESN'T EVEN KNOW WHERE THEY'RE GOING... HOW DOES HE KNOW HE WANTS TO GO THERE?
BECAUSE WHEREVER IT IS, IT'S NOT HERE.
ISN'T THAT THE SADDEST THING YOU'VE EVER SEEN?
NO.
TAKE MEEEEEE
WHAM
IT'S WHEN HE RUNS INTO THE TELEPHONE POLES.
Hospital. Take Me.

You know, this has nothing to do with this particular strip, but I just want to say that now that I've told you about the snakes in the toilet thing, you're gonna think about it the next few times you go to the bathroom. Especially if you're going to the bathroom *while* you're reading this book.

You know, you really shouldn't be reading my book while you're going to the bathroom. It doesn't feel right.

WHAT ARE YOU DOING, RAT?

I'VE STARTED SELLING STOCK IN YOU. TODAY'S THE INITIAL PUBLIC OFFERING...HOW MUCH WOULD YOU LIKE TO BUY?

BUY STOCK in PIG! Ticker Symbol: DUMB

NONE. I'M A TOTAL FAILURE.

THAT WILL NOT LOOK GOOD IN THE PROSPECTUS.

WHATEVER HAPPENED TO MIKE, THAT FRIEND OF YOURS WHO WAS THE REAL ESTATE AGENT?

HE DIED. HE WAS WAITING TO MEET A FRIEND ON THE CORNER OF MAIN AND THIRD AND A BUS HIT HIM. THE SAD PART WAS, THEY USUALLY MET AT A DIFFERENT SPOT.

LOCATION. LOCATION. LOCATION.

Unlike when I got all the complaints for my "twin-killing" joke back in July, I didn't get a single complaint for this strip where a real estate agent dies. This is conclusive proof that real estate agents are less popular than twins.

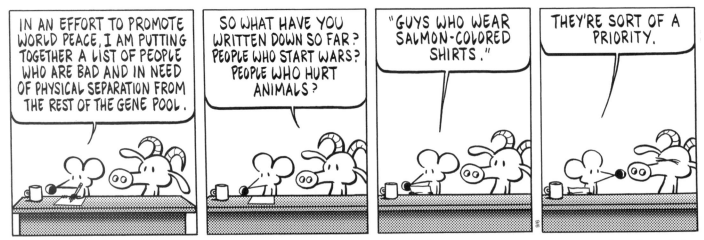

IN AN EFFORT TO PROMOTE WORLD PEACE, I AM PUTTING TOGETHER A LIST OF PEOPLE WHO ARE BAD AND IN NEED OF PHYSICAL SEPARATION FROM THE REST OF THE GENE POOL.

SO WHAT HAVE YOU WRITTEN DOWN SO FAR? PEOPLE WHO START WARS? PEOPLE WHO HURT ANIMALS?

"GUYS WHO WEAR SALMON-COLORED SHIRTS."

THEY'RE SORT OF A PRIORITY.

I wrote this in a café while sitting next to a guy in a salmon-colored shirt. At one point, it appeared as though he looked down at my notes. He didn't react, so I doubt he saw what I wrote. Then again, maybe he went home and cried.

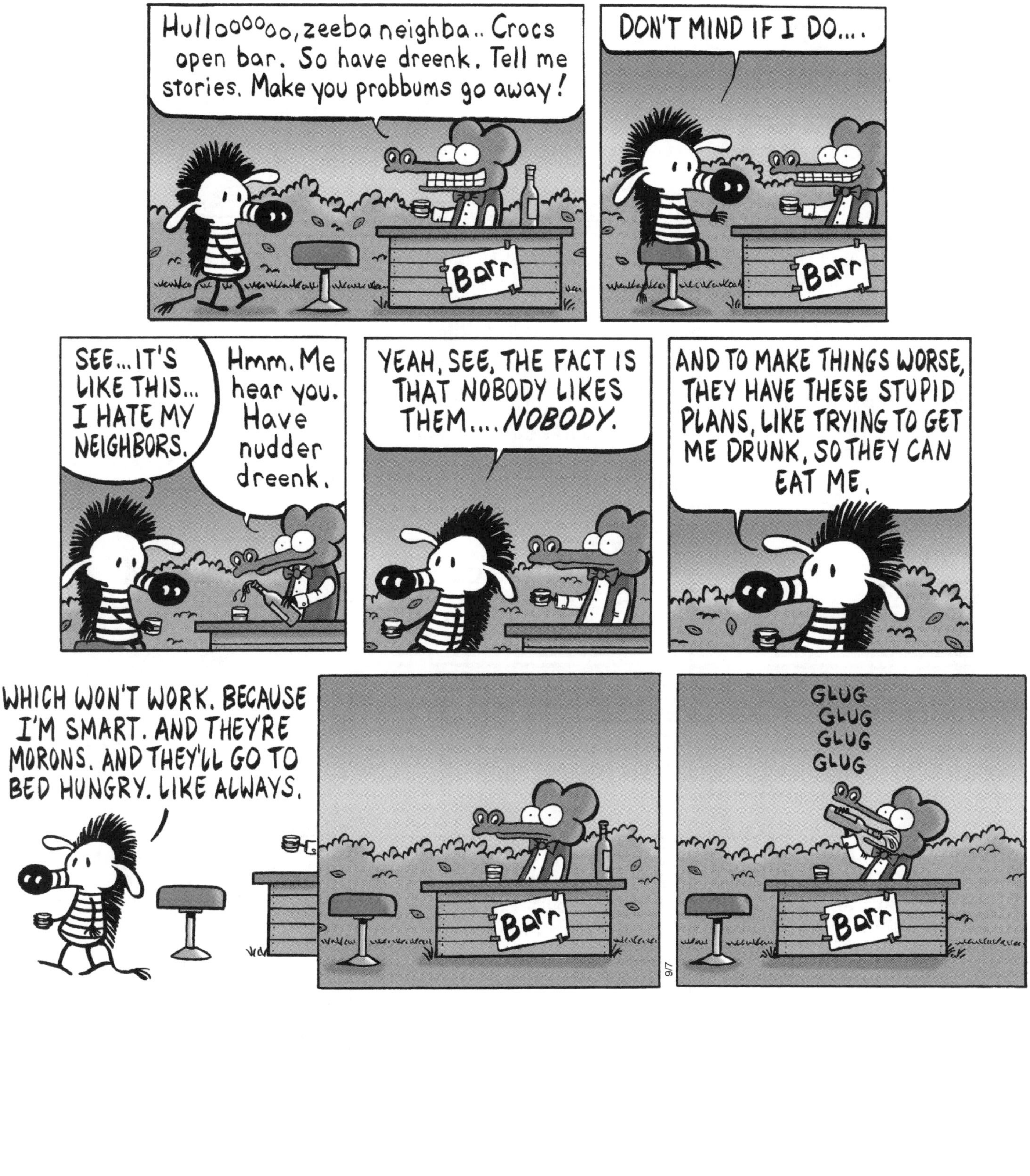
Hulloooooo, zeeba neighba.. Crocs open bar. So have dreenk. Tell me stories. Make you probbums go away!
DON'T MIND IF I DO....
Barr
SEE... IT'S LIKE THIS... I HATE MY NEIGHBORS.
Hmm. Me hear you. Have nudder dreenk.
YEAH, SEE, THE FACT IS THAT NOBODY LIKES THEM.... *NOBODY*.
AND TO MAKE THINGS WORSE, THEY HAVE THESE STUPID PLANS, LIKE TRYING TO GET ME DRUNK, SO THEY CAN EAT ME.
WHICH WON'T WORK. BECAUSE I'M SMART. AND THEY'RE MORONS. AND THEY'LL GO TO BED HUNGRY. LIKE ALWAYS.
GLUG GLUG GLUG GLUG

After I drew this strip, I called Brian Walker, the creator of *Hi and Lois,* and asked if there was any way he could do a strip about Castro on the day this strip was scheduled to run. Thus, anyone seeing the punch line in *Pearls* and then reading *Hi and Lois* would find that, indeed, this was a premise you could find in *Hi and Lois.* Brian agreed, and thus the *Hi and Lois* that ran on September 8, 2008 was about Castro.

I had a chance to go to Cuba with Jean Schulz (widow of Charles Schulz) in January 2010, but I wasn't able to make it. Half of me feared an angry Cuban customs agent with this week of strips taped to his customs booth saying, "We've been waiting for you."

When I originally drew Snuffle's "cigarette," I gave it a pointed little end, but I knew that wouldn't fly with my syndicate, so I changed it back into a more conventional cigarette shape.

For those who don't know, the lines in the last panel are from the Bob Marley song "I Shot the Sheriff."

I'm often asked why Pig wears this hat in the summer. The clever answer is that my strip runs in places in the Southern Hemisphere, like Australia, for whom our summer is their winter, and I have to be sensitive to that. The real answer is that I usually draw the strips nine months ahead of when they'll appear, and when I lay them out for publication, I pay very little attention to what season it may or may not be. (I should probably stick with the Australia answer.)

Isn't this what most everyone who goes to a family therapist secretly wishes?

I like Rat's little "Tee hee hee."

This came from a televangelist I saw praying over a pile of contributions people had sent him and blessing everyone who had sent him money.

Rat was originally saying, "Be cheap and I escort you to a life in hell." But the word "hell" is occasionally problematic, so I wussed out and changed it to what you see here. At this rate, my strip will be nothing but rainbows and smiley faces by the time I'm seventy.

HI, FOLKS, IT'S ME, RAT. THINK THE COMICS ARE JUST FOR YUCKS? THINK ONLY 'DOONESBURY' DOES SOCIAL COMMENTARY? WELL, YOU'RE WRONG.

THE TRUTH IS, SYNDICATED CARTOONISTS ARE DOING SOCIAL AND POLITICAL COMMENTARY IN THEIR COMICS ALMOST EVERY DAY. YOU'RE JUST NOT SEEING IT.

DON'T BELIEVE ME? WHY JUST LOOK AT THIS 'HAGAR THE HORRIBLE.' THE SYMBOLISM IS, OF COURSE, OBVIOUS. BUT FOR THOSE OF YOU THAT CAN'T SEE IT, I'VE PROVIDED SOME HELPFUL NOTES.

APOLOGIES TO THE GREAT CHRIS BROWNE

SPECIAL THANKS TO BRENDAN BURFORD.

HAGAR THE HORRIBLE Chris Browne

I HAPPEN TO KNOW YOU CAN BUY THIS HOUSE AT A VERY GOOD PRICE!

WHY

THEY'RE SELLING IT "AS IS"

Here we have a commentary on the various religious sects fighting for power in Iraq. Hagar, representing the Sunni minority in Baghdad, is returning to a neighborhood destroyed by sectarian violence.

The real estate agent, a metaphor for the radical Shiite cleric Muqtada al-Sadr (note the all-black coat) is attempting to lure Hagar into a poorly-protected home, an obvious trap.

Helga, who symbolizes the ineffective Nouri al-Maliki regime, stands passively by, unwilling or unable to help Hagar.

Do the sects resolve their differences? Of course not, as illustrated by the gathering clouds in the distance.

JOIN ME NEXT WEEK AS I REVEAL THE CONNECTION BETWEEN GARFIELD'S LASAGNA AND THE RE-EMERGENCE OF THE TOTALITARIAN STATE IN RUSSIA.

9/21

Because I was reprinting an actual *Hagar the Horrible* here, I called *Hagar*'s creator, Chris Browne, and asked if it was okay. I have to say it's rather awkward to open a conversation with the creator of *Hagar the Horrible* by saying, "Hi, I'm Stephan Pastis and I want to analyze how your strip is a metaphor for the sectarian violence in Iraq." But he was very nice and let me do it.

"Shelter from the Storm" is a Bob Dylan song. It's from a Dylan album called *Blood on the Tracks*. If I could only take five albums to a desert island, *Blood on the Tracks* would definitely be one of them. Then again, I doubt the island would have a power source, so I'd probably just end up staring at the album cover.

It looks like I'm using a ruler for the rain again, but now I'm using a thinner pen, so it actually looks okay. At this rate, I will be a great artist by the time I'm seventy. Of course, none of that will matter because my strip will be nothing but rainbows and smiley faces.

ISN'T IT AMAZING THAT THE BUSINESS WORLD, GENERALLY KNOWN FOR ITS NO-NONSENSE PRAGMATISM, IS CENTERED IN SKYSCRAPERS THAT HAVE NO THIRTEENTH FLOORS?

WHY DON'T THEY HAVE THIRTEENTH FLOORS?

SUPERSTITION. ISN'T THAT AMAZING?

YEAH, BUT WHAT'S EVEN MORE AMAZING IS HOW THEY RIP OUT THE THIRTEENTH FLOOR WITHOUT THE REST OF THE BUILDING FALLING DOWN.

PERHAPS I'LL KEEP MY KEEN INSIGHTS TO MYSELF.

THAT'S ONE SERIOUS GAME OF JENGA.

I was surprised to get e-mails from some readers saying they'd never heard of Jenga. Jenga's a great game where you try to pull narrow wooden blocks from a tower without toppling it.

THE CROCODILE CHASES HIS ZEBRA PREY TO A DARK CORNER OF THE SWAMP. THE DOOMED ZEBRA IS TRAPPED, HEMMED IN BY A HIGH BANK.

LIKE ALL GOOD PREDATORS, THE CROC HAS SEARCHED FOR JUST THIS KIND OF OPPORTUNITY TO TRAP HIS PREY IN TIGHT QUARTERS.

WHAT ARE YOU DOING, PIG?

LOOKING THROUGH THE PHONE BOOK FOR A DENTIST TO CLEAN MY TEETH.

USE MY GUY. HE'S GOOD.

NO, I ONLY LIKE FEMALE DENTISTS TO WORK ON MY TEETH.

WHAT DIFFERENCE DOES IT MAKE?

IT'S THE CLOSEST I GET TO A WOMAN ALL YEAR.

At the time I did this strip, I had a female dentist, but I figured she never read the strip so it didn't matter. Then one day I walked in for a cleaning, and she handed me one of my books to sign. Now that I think about it, she's probably gonna see this comment too, so maybe I should just stop talking.

I goofed in the second-to-last panel by making the croc's head pop out over the speech balloon. It's a goof because it inadvertently makes it seem like the croc's head is coming through the closed window. Then again, maybe you didn't notice it, in which case you should just erase my comment from your head.

This triggered a flood of sarcastic e-mails from readers "thanking" me for planting this little song in their head. Now it's in yours, too. Ha ha ha!

I live in California and was surprised to hear from people in other parts of the country telling me they had never seen these little semicircles printed on the ground outside of doors. At every school I've ever been to in California, these semicircles are painted outside the door to warn people not to stand there, because the door opens out and could hit them. But I guess they're not universal. The things you learn.

As a former defense lawyer, I think I'm biased about how some people use the justice system.

If you look carefully at the Wheel o' Possible Defendants, you'll see me, Jerry Scott (co-creator of *Zits*), and Ron O' Neal, who is one of the salesmen for my syndicate.

I've drawn a number of "Neighbor Bobs" over the years, but I think I change his appearance every time. Maybe one of you is ambitious enough to create a collage of all the Neighbor Bobs I've drawn over the years so that I can see whether or not the look of the character is consistent. Then again, maybe you're just as lazy as me and have already turned the page.

I did not hear from Anderson Cooper after this strip ran. Maybe he's sensitive about his weasel-like laugh. Perhaps I'll make fun of his tight t-shirts next.

My baseball homage to *Peanuts*. In addition to the mound and flying clothes, I also modeled all the baseball caps in this series after the ones Schulz drew.

If I can get credit for one thing in the history of newspaper comics, I want it to be for my renaming testicles "oompa loompas."

Again, I think I went to the well one too many times with this kind of cat joke. Perhaps I felt it was okay to be trite one day after I pioneered a new use for the words "oompa loompas."

It appears this was Testicles Week in *Pearls*.

Gotta bring back the moles.

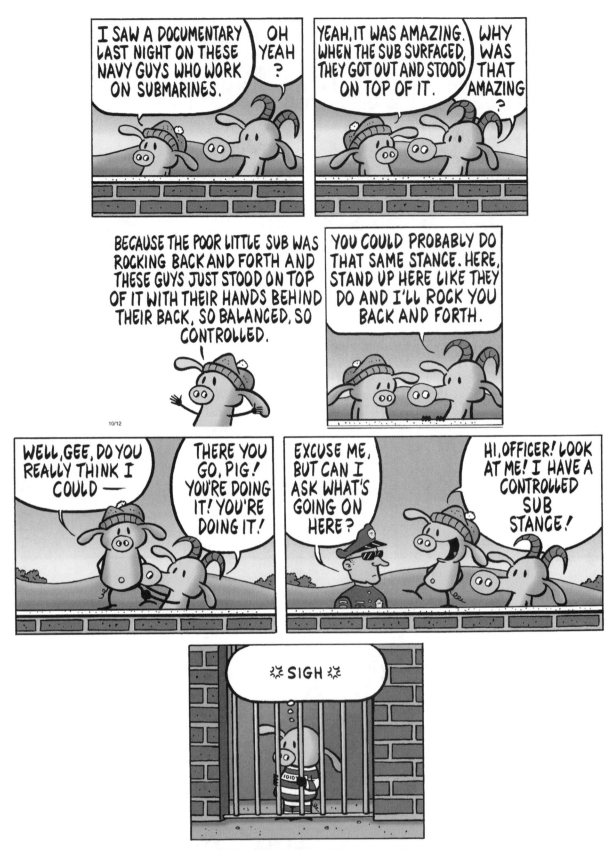

That cop is either 3 feet tall or standing in a hole. I'll let you pick.

I'm often asked to bring back a whole bunch of different characters who have appeared in past strips. So I thought I'd use this storyline to do it.

Here I am warning of the dangers of chewing tobacco, and I have three characters in my strip who smoke cigarettes (me, Rat, and Guard Duck).

This must have been very strange for newer readers who had never seen Toby the Agoraphobic Turtle before. But strange never stops me. I thrive on strange.

113

I'm fairly certain the baseball games in *Peanuts* weren't played to the death. But then again, the characters of Shermy and Violet did seem to disappear at some point in the strip.

If those croc baseball poses look better than poses I can draw, it's because they are. I copied them straight out of *Peanuts*.

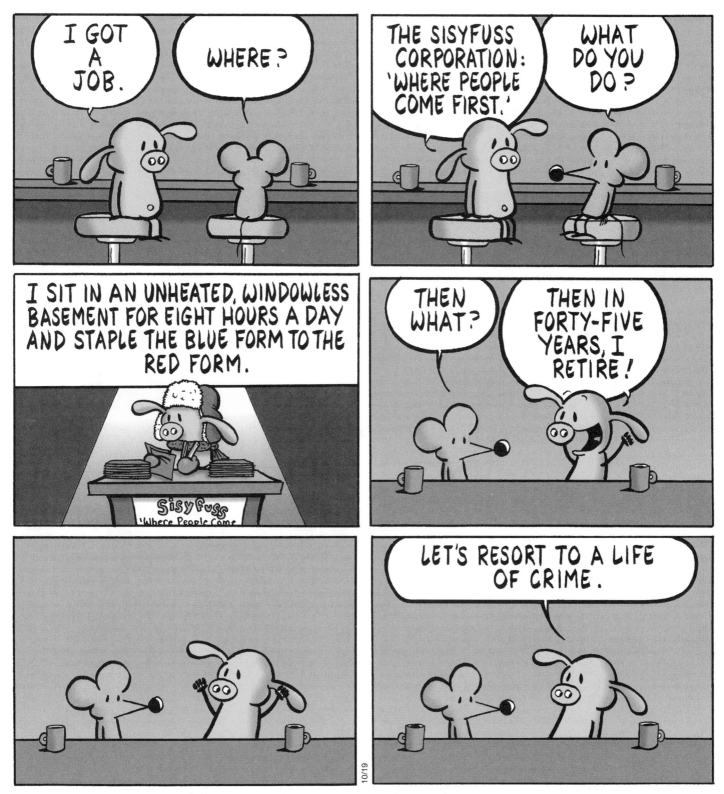

When I look back at this image of Pig sitting at his desk in his *Fargo* hat, I now see it was directly inspired by the character of Ignatius J. Reilly in the novel *A Confederacy of Dunces*, a book I will once again say is the funniest I have ever read.

Since I got so many requests to bring back this whale character who had died in the strip two years earlier, I thought I'd finally do it. Here at Pearls, Inc., we put the reader first.

Although I have to agree with Rat, I miss Gary Larson (*The Far Side*) even more.

Look at what a suck-up I am. Between the panels, I wrote, "Apologies to the ever-patient and beautiful Cathy Guisewite." I must have thought she was going to sue me.

Take *that*, all you whining over-sensitive buttheads who wrote to complain about Andy being on that chain! He winds up the hero!

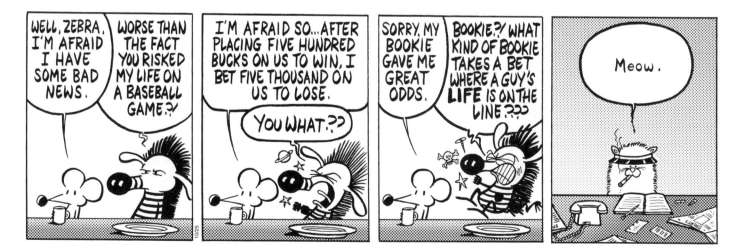

I don't even know what Baroque music is. I just know it worked for the pun.

This came from a trip I took with my son to a place called Safari West in Santa Rosa, California. They have all these great animals, including a fennec fox. What Pig says about their hearing is supposedly true.

I wrote "HAM" on that ham so you'd know it was ham. I'd write it on every difficult-to-draw-object in the strip, but it would probably look odd to have a table with "TABLE" written on it.

I often find myself having to write strips on days that I'm depressed. This must have been one such day.

I was lucky enough to go to a party at *Cathy* creator Cathy Guisewite's house during the 2009 Reubens in Los Angeles (the Reubens are like the Oscars of cartooning). It was a Mexican-themed party, and I walked around the entire time in a giant sombrero that I took off one of the tables. I have not been invited back.

I have never been so under-the-influence of any drug that I saw flying bunnies. Though I once thought I could fly.

Do the backs of *any* TVs look like this anymore? I need to update my cultural reference points.

And what TVs still have rabbit ears? Seriously, it's like 1977 in this strip. I'm now ashamed.

I was surprised (and a little depressed) by the number of people who didn't know this was a reference to John Steinbeck's *The Grapes of Wrath*.

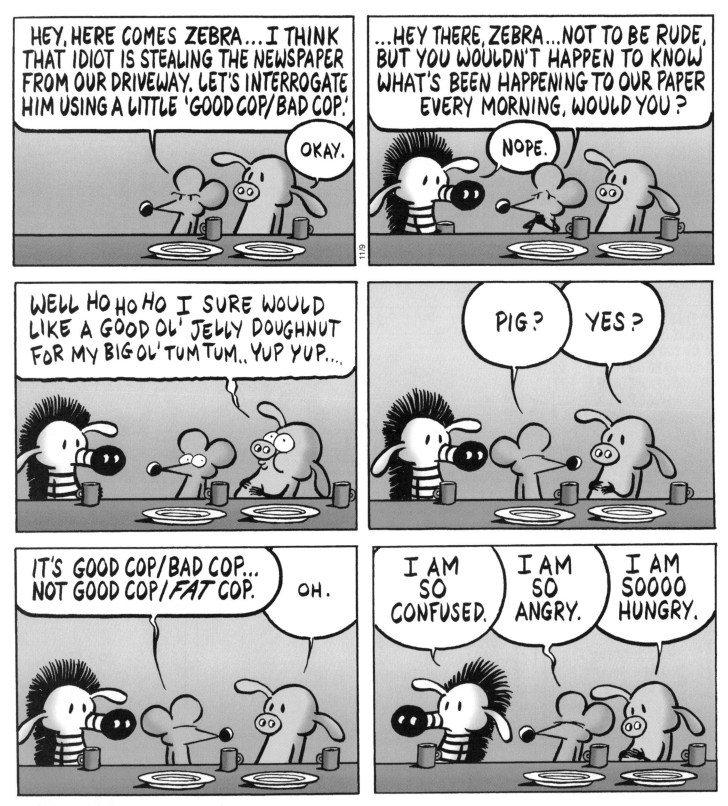

This strip came from a conversation my son was having with his friend in the back seat of my car when I was driving them to school. One of them mentioned "good cop/bad cop," and the other, not knowing the reference, asked, "What's good cop/fat cop?"

That's supposed to be me without my usual backwards cap in the last panel.

Okay, isn't this Burger King slogan also from the 1970s? Are *all* my references from that decade?

This was a very popular strip. (Really, I'm not making this one up.)

When you're short of comic ideas, just kick someone in the oompa loompas.

This strip, the 11/12 strip ("We were so ahead of our time"), and the 11/7 strip (the Joads) were all written about the time when it looked like we were headed for another Great Depression in the fall of 2008. Because I'm generally eight months ahead of deadline, I subbed them all in so they would run while all that was happening, rather than nine months later.

And now *I'm* that guy with the unclever blog (www.stephanpastis.wordpress.com). With plugs like that, who needs detractors?

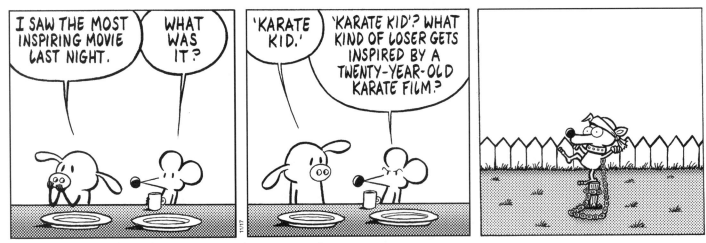

Hey, a reference from the 1980s. I'm becoming relevant.

I like saying, "Shut your pieholes," because it sounds a lot dirtier than it is.

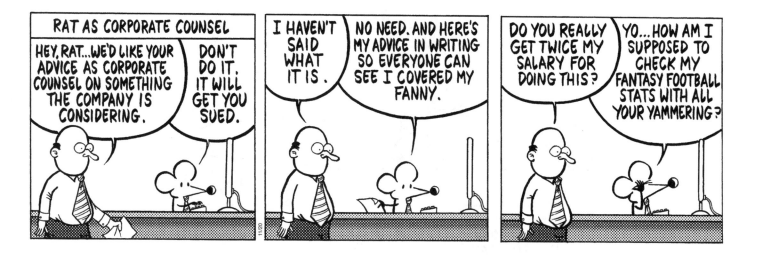

And yet this would still be a better religion than a lot of the ones out there.

Ironically, this strip itself is now on a dental reminder postcard.

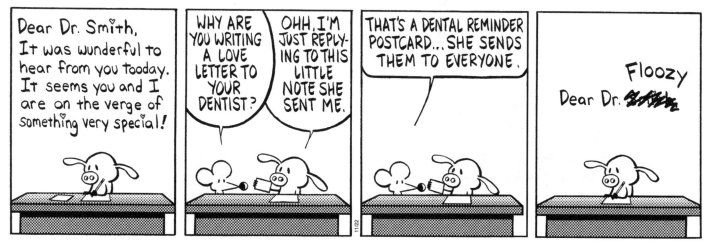

Why am I so obsessed with the names "Bob" and "Larry"? It can't be healthy.

This was a very popular strip, proving that perky people are a despised race.

I wanted to use a line from Shakespeare that was totally incomprehensible. To find it, all I had to do was open one of his plays and point to any page.

This was a series I had drawn a few years before but just never ran. You can tell by how different the characters look.

Comic strip artists always use the same old swear squiggles (e.g., a star, a lightning bolt, a screw, Saturn, a number sign), so I wanted to originate one myself. Thus, I invented the Darby. The Darby is the little face you see in those swear squiggles in the first and second panels, and it's supposed to look like *Get Fuzzy* cartoonist Darby Conley. Unfortunately, the Darby never caught on.

A couple more Darbys.

I showed this to some cartoonists before running it, and the consensus was that I shouldn't publish it because it was too mean-spirited toward some of the older cartoonists. I ignored their advice and ran it anyway. Ironically, while I got no complaints about my treatment of the older cartoonists, I *did* get a lot of complaints about the supposed death of Danny Donkey.

You can't go wrong making a "Kumbaya" reference. It's comedy gold.

Take a moment to admire those tire tracks. They're well drawn.

For those who don't know, this is a reference to the famous "bed-in" by John Lennon and Yoko Ono, when they stayed in their bed for a week to promote peace around the world.

The "big, tasty Kahuna burger" is a reference to the fictional brand of burgers used in Quentin Tarantino's films. Aren't you glad you have me along to explain all of these obscure references?

When I do strips like this, I simply go to Google Images and look up Elizabethan clothing. I can't imagine what it was like to work as a cartoonist before the Internet. I know from looking at Charles Schulz's personal library that he had to have hundreds of reference books on all sorts of topics. Now you just need an Internet connection.

Look at that drawing of the Kremlin in the background. It's so realistic you'd think you were looking at a photograph.

The size of this missile really varies from strip to strip. I can't explain that.

137

Looking at the useless pan and football helmet on the characters' heads, I'm reminded of the nuclear attack drills we used to have to do in grade school, where an alarm would go off and we'd duck below our desks. Because everyone knows a nuclear bomb can't touch you if you're protected by a third-grader's school desk.

Goat is reading *Master of the Senate* by Robert Caro. It's one in a series of books Caro has written about Lyndon Johnson. It's the greatest biography I've ever read.

The introduction of Elly Elephant. She's named after my niece, Elenique.

As useful as hiding below a third-grader's desk.

Banging on things is always my Plan B for fixing anything.

Man, I went to a lot of trouble to draw that column, and it really adds nothing to the joke. I am not a smart man.

Here I return to the missile storyline. I like to do stuff like this, where I interrupt a storyline to go to a second storyline, and then merge the two together. Otherwise, when you run the same storyline for ten straight days, you run the risk of boring readers. Like I just did with this comment.

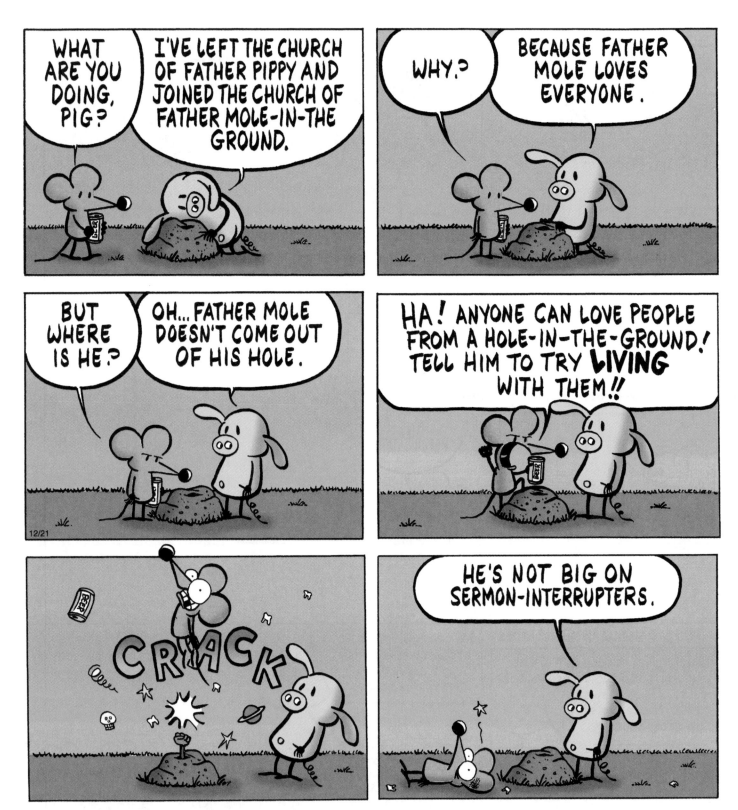

I'm with Rat here. It's a lot easier to love other people if you don't have to live with other people.

I once drove in a car from the state of Washington into Canada, and I have to say, I have never been so grilled by a border agent as I was that day going into Canada. Perhaps they've had a bad experience with syndicated cartoonists.

Another case of my deleting the word "hell" and replacing it with a euphemistic phrase, in this case, "that big, fiery place."

143

I really thought I'd get some serious flak from some folk about this reference to the Rapture, so I ran it on Christmas, in the hopes that fewer people would see it. Christmas may be the greatest of all days to hide a crappy strip.

This is a reference to the final scene in Stanley Kubrick's film *Dr. Strangelove*. I liked the image enough to make it the cover of the 2011 *Pearls* desk calendar.

And thus I merge the preacher and missile storylines. I applaud my own cleverosity.

I have to bring back Maura every now and again.

When I was a kid, I loved Christmas. As an adult, I see it more as an interruption in my routine. Other than watching my kids open their presents, I really don't enjoy it.

This is me at parties. Strangely, I don't get invited back to a lot of them.

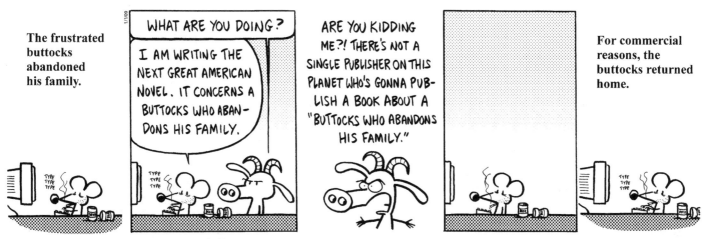

The frustrated buttocks abandoned his family.

WHAT ARE YOU DOING?

I AM WRITING THE NEXT GREAT AMERICAN NOVEL. IT CONCERNS A BUTTOCKS WHO ABANDONS HIS FAMILY.

ARE YOU KIDDING ME?! THERE'S NOT A SINGLE PUBLISHER ON THIS PLANET WHO'S GONNA PUBLISH A BOOK ABOUT A "BUTTOCKS WHO ABANDONS HIS FAMILY."

For commercial reasons, the buttocks returned home.

This is another really old series that I didn't love, so I delayed running it. I finally decided to run it around New Year's, assuming again that fewer people would be reading their paper. I have to say, though, looking back at these strips now, I kinda like a couple of them.

The buttocks hated the holidays, for holidays meant family. And there was nothing worse than a family of buttocksesses.

I'M SORRY, RAT...I DON'T MEAN TO BE A CRITIC... BUT THERE'S NO SUCH THING AS A "FAMILY OF BUTTOCKSESSES."

~~buttocksesses.~~
butti

Despondent, the buttocks wept.

HOW NICE...YOU'RE STILL WRITING A NOVEL WITH A "BUTTOCKS" FOR A PROTAGONIST...GEE, WHY DON'T YOU WRITE A REALLY AMBIGUOUS ENDING WHERE YOUR DESPONDENT BUTTOCKS DRIVES HIS CAR OFF A CLIFF? DID HE DO IT INTENTIONALLY? DID HE SECRETLY *WANT* TO DIE? GOSH, WHO KNOWS? IT'S A MASTERPIECE. THEY *ALL* HAVE AMBIGUOUS ENDINGS...WE CAN DEBATE IT FOR YEARS.

NO TRUE LITERARY GENIUS HAS EVER ESCAPED THE CONTEMPT OF HIS PEERS... I DO NOT EXPECT MY SITUATION TO BE DIFFERENT... NOW RUN ALONG.

Mocking the warning of the certified Midas brake specialist, the buttocks drove to the mountains.

Holy smokes. Way too many words. You know a comic's not good when there's no room for the pictures.

I really liked how the image in the fifth panel turned out. A rare moment of romantic bliss in *Pearls*.

Having taken this vacation to Cancun, I can vouch for its expensiveness.

At the time of writing this strip, I had just finished reading a biography of the great architect Frank Lloyd Wright. It had a big impact on me. But no, he never built an office building out of rotating cheese.

If you look at the buildings in the drawing Pig is holding, you'll see that one of them is the cheese building referenced in the prior strip. That, my friends, is plot coherence.

So here I am talking about deleting panel lines, but if you look at the strip I'm drawing on the desk, there are panel lines. So much for plot coherence.

Not sure why, but "begonias" is a funnier word than "daisies" or "sunflowers." I think Charles Schulz once said that "B" words are inherently funny.

That elephant came out pretty decent. I shall pat myself on the back.

This was one of the most popular strips of the year, particularly among librarians, many of whom told me they taped this strip to the checkout counter at their respective libraries.

Please note there are seven "beeps" and "boops" in the second panel, corresponding to the exact number of digits in a telephone number. That's the kind of attention to detail that makes me the cartoonist I am.

This strip should have been run on Earth Day, which is in April. Instead, I ran it in January. That's the kind of inattention to detail that makes me the cartoonist I am.

A very popular strip, so much so that I made the image in the second panel the cover of the 2011 *Pearls* wall calendar. (Hint, hint . . . There are *Pearls* wall calendars. Buy them so I can afford more trips to Cancun.)

This Fantastic Four series was really popular, but man, it took forever to draw these guys in their get-ups, particularly when it came to drawing staplers and doorstops on their heads. Next time I draw croc superheroes, their special powers will all involve invisibility.

Despite the premise stated in the first strip that there are only three of these Fantastic Four guys ("Math is not part of their fantasticalness"), I kept getting e-mails throughout the week saying things such as, "Dude, you keep calling these guys the Fantastic Four, but there are only three of them."

If something I own doesn't work, I will try and see if I can fix it. But if thirty seconds pass and it's still not working, I will hit or kick it. It doesn't help, but it feels great.

This strip got a big reaction. I guess I'm not the only one who thinks printer ink is a big rip-off.

That would be the Eiffel Tower and Arc de Triomphe on the wall behind them. That's how you know they're in Paris and not in, say, Pittsburgh.

I just went to Wikipedia and learned that ducks don't even have toes. So I'm not quite sure what it was that Snuffles was rubbing.

I put a beret on Guard Duck to remind you that he's in Paris, because everyone knows that every single French person wears a beret. I should mention here that everything I ever learned about French people came from watching Pepé Le Pew cartoons.

A very, very, very old cartoon that I waited a very, very, very long time to run, meaning I really, really, really didn't like it.

I had to call Sprint Directory Services ten times to get what the recording was saying in Spanish. My wife, Staci, later showed me that each call cost fifty cents. So this strip is worth at least $5.

Whuh ees you reading son?

A BOOK ON MARTIN LUTHER KING, JR... I'M TRYING TO READ BOOKS ABOUT ALL MY HEROES, LIKE KING AND LINCOLN AND GANDHI AND TOLSTOY.

HEH HEH HEH... Ohhhhh, son... You call *dem* heroes??

OF COURSE I CALL THEM HEROES. WHO DO *YOU* CONSIDER HEROES?

I SURE MISS MY L'IL GUARD DUCK.

HOW'S THAT LITTLE MILITARY WINGNUT DOING?

HE'S SO IN LOVE. HE AND MAURA NEVER EVEN LEAVE THEIR APARTMENT... THEY WANT TO SPEND EVERY MINUTE TOGETHER.

WHAT'S A GUY LIKE HIM DO ALL DAY WITH A GIRLFRIEND?

KAMCHATKA IS MINE!

My Risk strategy does not involve Kamchatka, but it does involve Siam. I will say no more.

WHAT'S THE MATTER TODAY, MAURA? YOU'RE NOT INVADING SIAM WITH YOUR USUAL FLAIR.

QUACK

'WE HAVE TO TALK'? 'WE HAVE TO TALK'? YOU JUST SAID, 'WE HAVE TO TALK.'...

QUACK

NO, THEY'RE NOT JUST WORDS... THEY'RE BIG WORDS... **HUGE** WORDS... BIG, HUGE WORDS THAT HAUL **DOOM**!

WHY, THEY'RE THE FOUR WORDSMEN OF THE APOCALYPSE!!

HOP HOP HOP HOP

YOU WERE SAYING...?

I really only draw Guard Duck in one pose, which is standing in profile with his mouth closed. Thus, whenever I have to draw a strip like this where he's animated and jumping around, it's a challenge.

The "clean, well-lighted" phrase comes from the title of my favorite short story by Ernest Hemingway, "A Clean, Well-Lighted Place."

If I can say this without seeming like an enormous ass, I'm very proud of the writing in this strip. I'd have to put it in my personal Top Five for *Pearls* strips.

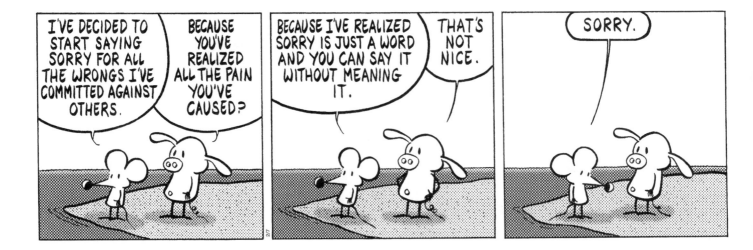

Oddly enough, the idea for this strip came from my mom, who always underlines certain words in the Hallmark birthday cards she sends me. Granted, they're usually words like "love" and "proud," and not "You . . . break . . . wind."

The number on the prisoner's chest (0116) is my birthday (January 16). These are the things I do to amuse myself.

Sometimes when I'm trying to fall asleep late at night, I become acutely aware of my heart beating, and I ponder how easily it could stop beating. It makes for a long night.

On the morning this strip appeared in papers, I got a nice e-mail from historian John Barry himself thanking me for the mention. I sent him the original, and he sent me a signed copy of one of his books. Too bad this trick never works with supermodels.

I have never owned a bird. That's not that interesting, but when you have to fill an entire book with commentary, you sometimes reach.

My five-panel strips are rarely very good. I think the very fact that I'm having to use five panels (as opposed to the usual three) means I don't have my usual timing down in the writing process.

I had just turned forty years old when I wrote this, so I can only assume it was the inspiration for this strip. It's odd, but in my head I'm about seventeen, so I'm always shocked when a birthday rolls around and I'm reminded of my real age.

Sentimental strips like this really throw people for a loop, because I think they expect me to *always* be dark and cynical. But I try not to overdo the sentimental thing, because I think there's too much of it on the comics page. Also, when you do it as rarely as I do, I think it has more of an impact.

This turned out to be a very popular strip. Ironically, I was not a hockey fan at the time I wrote it but have since become one, largely due to the success of our local team, the San Jose Sharks.

I'm often tempted to make Rat's persona here a recurring gag, where he would go around beating up other comic strip characters who were not funny that day.

I am now told by my book publisher that this is not how you spell "okay doke." They wanted to correct it, but I said no, only because I like the strips in the book to appear just as they did in the newspapers.

168

THE ADVENTURES OF ANGRY BOB

Angry Bob was angry.

"I will go to a children's soccer game," said Bob, "Childhood sports make people happy."

So Angry Bob went to a game. He stood on the sidelines. He stood with the parents of a team called "The Strikers."

The Strikers were losing. The parents were angry. They yelled. One swore.

So Angry Bob stood in front of them.

"Rejoice," he said, raising his arms in celebration, "for the goal of childhood sport is not victory, but rather, the inculcation of values such as teamwork, fair play and the struggle to do one's best."

A Gatorade bottle struck Bob in the head.

Falling, Bob saw a horde of angry soccer moms descend upon his fragile bean.

"You Strikers," he said with his last breath, "are aptly named."

HELL HATH NO FURY LIKE A LOSING SOCCER MOM.

I wrote this at my son's soccer game. "The Strikers" was his team's name. I wouldn't have known if the other parents were angry or yelling because I sit around 50 yards away from everyone else, listening to my iPod and occasionally writing ideas (such as this one) in my notebook. They must think I'm the Unabomber.

I had a ton of fun writing these next three strips. I got to look up all these Yiddish words online and pick the ones I wanted to give to Rat. I also learned in the process that Yiddish truly does have the greatest insults of any language. It seemed like every other word meant "idiot." It's Rat's dream language.

I have to say that I was a little worried that one of the words I chose would actually have an inappropriate meaning I didn't intend. So I tried to look up each of the words on multiple Internet sites to make sure their definition was agreed-upon and safe.

Another very popular strip. Man, I was on quite a streak. Of course, I'll suck later on in this book, so don't get too excited.

I was fascinated by the *Guinness Book of World Records* as a kid and would memorize the names of the tallest guy, the fattest guy, and the guy who could shove the most cigarettes in his mouth.

Somewhere between panels 1 and 3, Larry must have downed another beer, because there's an extra beer on the floor in panel 3. Either that or the idiot who drew it wasn't paying attention.

This is my tribute to my Yiayia Pana, who had big, jiggly arms I used to sleep against. *Yiayia* is Greek for "grandma."

I'm at the point now where I can barely watch the news at night. It gets me too depressed. Not so much for the content of the news but for the idiotic and simplistic way it's presented.

If you look carefully, you'll see the ninja suits they're wearing here are different from the ones in the 3/3 strip. The prior suits did not cover the crocs' snouts. I had to do that because in the prior strip I needed the croc to be able to drink that milkshake, and if his entire mouth was covered that wouldn't be possible. Oh, how smart I am.

I interspersed these two storylines (the hippo one and the ninja one) because I knew I was going to merge them at the end of the week. Of course, if you were someone who just picked up the comics for the first time this day, you'd have no idea what the last panel was supposed to mean.

174

One of my friends named Sean asked to be in one of my comics. He's a San Diego Chargers fan. So I put him in the fourth panel and put a crudely drawn Chargers logo on his tie. I also had Danny Donkey telling him to shut his mouth, which is probably not the depiction he was hoping for. But those are the risks you run when you ask to be included in a *Pearls* comic.

I think every one of Rat's neighbors is bald. As is most every man I draw in *Pearls*.

See, there's another one. It's ridiculous. I really do draw a lot of bald guys. Maybe I can get an endorsement deal from Hair Club for Men.

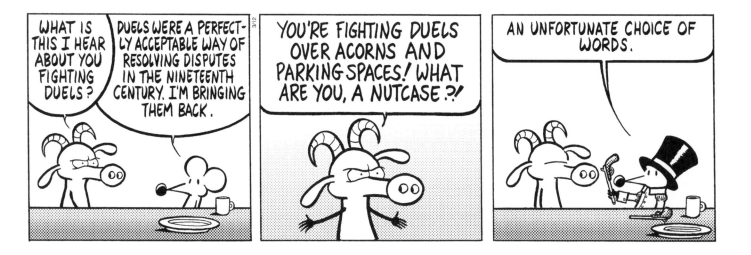

Okay, if you've been paying attention to the prior commentary in this book, you know that there are two key clues to the fact that the last panel is supposed to be set in Paris (and not Pittsburgh). I'll give you some time to think.

And the answer to the last comment is (a) The beret and (b) The fact that everyone is either making out with a girl or drinking. (And you thought it was the Eiffel Tower.)

177

I have to confess, I love listening to a director's commentary. It's the *actors'* commentary I can't stand. Why do we glamorize actors so much and pay so little attention to directors?

On the day this strip ran, I got a nice e-mail from the creator of *Garfield Minus Garfield*. He also sent me a book of his strips. It's really funny stuff, and if you've never read it, you should.

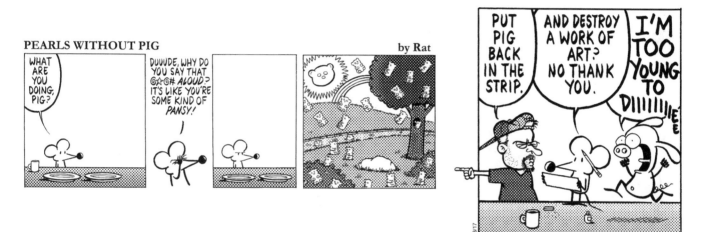

After this strip ran, I invited readers of my blog to create their own *Pearls* strips where they removed one or more characters from the strip. Sadly, it improved many of my strips.

At my law firm, we used to have seminars on Friday mornings, and someone would always have to bring in donuts. Me and another attorney always used to fight over the sprinkled ones, which sometimes he would grab from my hand before I could take a bite. So I started the practice of licking them as soon as I got them. That might give you a clue as to why I'm no longer working at a law firm.

This was a popular strip, but one thing has always bugged me about it. And that is that in the last panel, it's not clear what's shoved up Pig's nose. It's supposed to be the rolled-up envelope, but I think it looks more like a thermometer or something. Maybe I should have written "rolled-up envelope" and drawn a little arrow to it.

This strip is more autobiographical than I'd care to admit.

I really did see this in the news. I thought it was perfect for a strip.

Unlike the hedgehog story, I just made up this employment statistic. That's the beauty of comic strips. You can just lie, lie, lie.

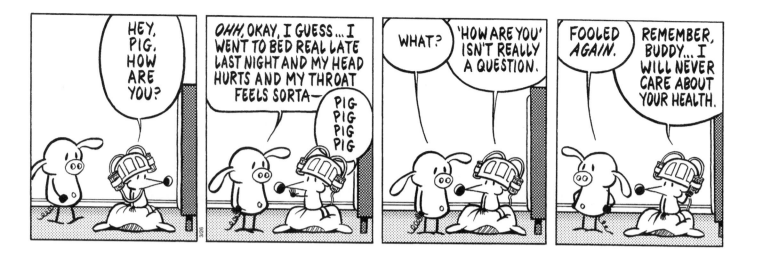

I had to go out of my way to say it was *tobacco* that Rat was smoking in his hookah pipe. Otherwise, it would have triggered complaints.

I must say, this is not a great strip. I encourage you to draw your own over it.

I thought I could get away without specifying tobacco here because I had already done it in the Friday strip (3/27). But I was wrong. Sure enough, people complained that Rat was smoking marijuana.

This is one of those occasions when Rat and I think exactly alike.

The TV, dresser, and bed are my way of telling you that Rat is staying in a hotel room. Had there been an Eiffel Tower in the background, you would have known that Rat was staying in Paris. It's little things like that which separate my comic from all the rest.

This was a much more popular strip than I thought it would be. I never seem to know which ones will resonate.

Looking back on it, I think this series was a little out of character for Zebra. It's a pretty aggressive act to kidnap someone else's wife, and he's just not that aggressive.

So here I establish that Larry can't read. And yet ten days ago (in the 3/25 strip), he was reading a newspaper. My explanation is that he drank so much beer on 4/3, he lost the ability to read.

That "CUPPA JOE CUPPA JOE" image was very popular, so we ended up putting it on coffee mugs. If the link still works, you can find it here: http://www.cafepress.com/comics.416416030.

Every time I look at Larry's "cons" list ("None me can tink of"), I laugh. I don't often laugh at my own strips.

Ohhh, man . . . more staplers . . . more doorstops. This is gonna be a long drawing week.

There was only one way I was gonna be able to save myself from having to draw these labor-intensive superheroes over and over. And that was to kill them off one by one.

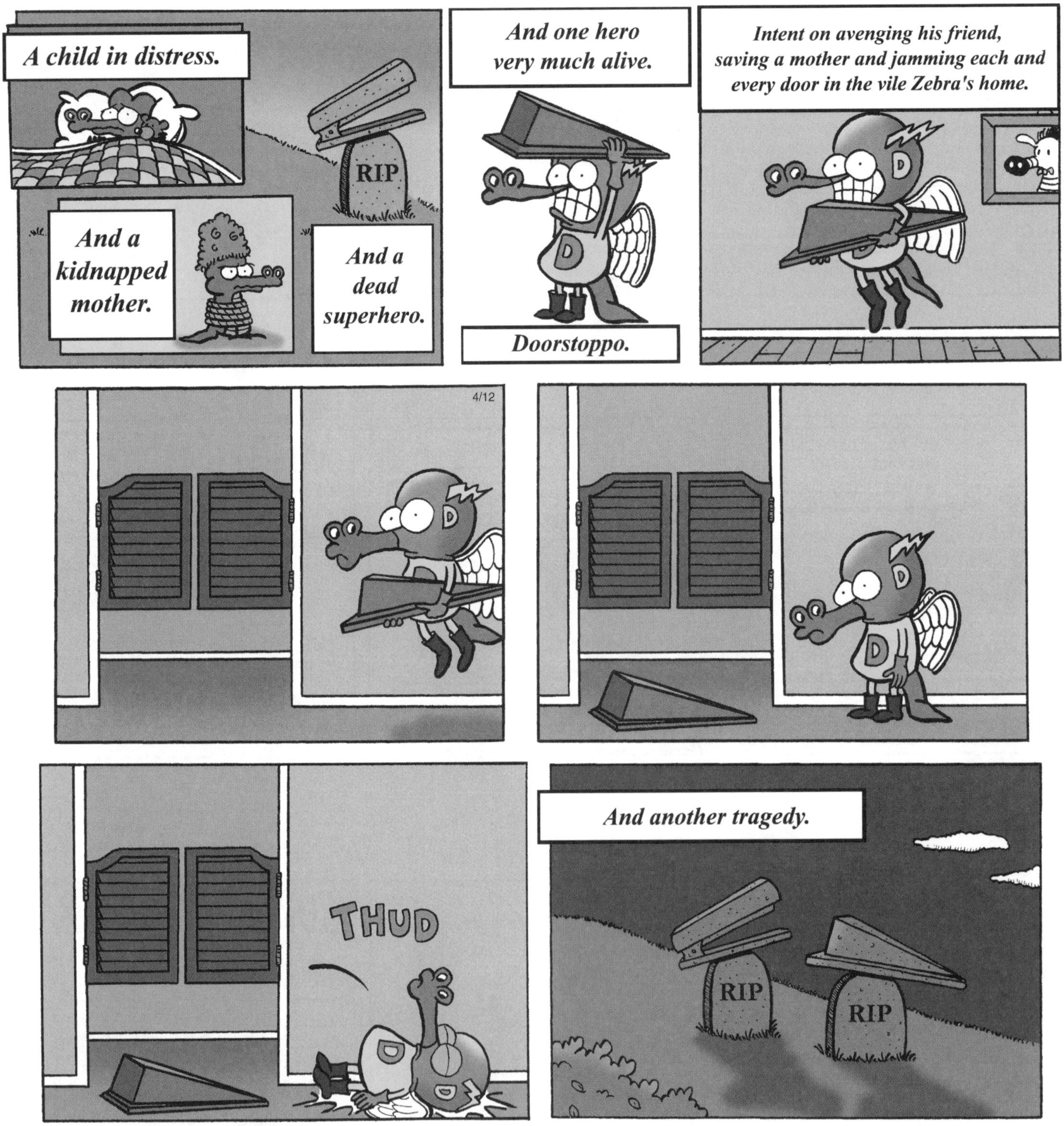
A child in distress.
RIP
And a kidnapped mother.
And a dead superhero.
And one hero very much alive.
Doorstoppo.
Intent on avenging his friend, saving a mother and jamming each and every door in the vile Zebra's home.
4/12
THUD
And another tragedy.
RIP
RIP

Two down. One to go.

Got him. My drawing hand thanks me.

If you look very carefully at Larry in the last panel, you'll see that he's guarding his "potatoes."

On nights when I have trouble sleeping, I often do what Pig is talking about in the second panel. It helps me to relax.

Maybe I'm too conspiratorially minded, but shortly after this strip appeared, I got a number of e-mails complaining about this strip, and all appeared to say the exact same thing, which was that the great fiscal crisis of 2008–2009 was not the banks' fault. Now I'm used to getting complaints, especially from boneheads, but what made these unusual was that the e-mails were *way* too similar to each other, indicating to me that they had been orchestrated by some person or organization. It was all very bizarre.

During my trip to Iraq in October 2009, I got to spend a fair amount of time with *Doonesbury* creator Garry Trudeau. After the trip, I sent him some *Pearls* books, as well as the original of this strip. I figured this particular strip was appropriate, as it concerned an issue near and dear to the both of us. In return, he sent me a great big box full of *Doonesbury* stuff, including a number of signed books. It was awesome.

This was based on the grave of Senator Roland Burris, the man who filled Barack Obama's Senate seat after Obama became president. If you've never seen it, just Google "Roland Burris" and "gravestone." Believe it or not, Burris (who's not yet dead but has already designed his own tombstone) had the word "Trailblazer" engraved on it. And you thought I just made this stuff up.

Imagine if you were a new *Pearls* reader and this was the first strip you ever saw. This used to happen a lot when a new paper would start running *Pearls* and just randomly begin the strip on whatever day they wanted. To prevent that, we now give each new paper an introductory set of strips that introduces all of the various characters. Otherwise, readers see a strip like this on the first day and ask themselves, "What the hell is going on?"

Shortly after this, the recession ended. I credit myself.

195

I draw way too many pillars. I'll stop eventually.

Shortly after drawing this strip (but before it appeared in papers), I saw this identical joke appear in Darrin Bell's comic strip *Candorville*. Because I knew mine would appear after his (and therefore look like I was ripping him off), I called Darrin and let him know I had done the strip before ever seeing his. In talking to him, I told him the dates my strips would run, and he had some fun with it by having Rat appear like a hobo in *his* strip on the very day my strip ran. It was great.

Furthering the crossover, Darrin had a naked Dennis the Menace appear in his strip on this day. Even better, he cleverly used his signature to obscure Dennis's private parts.

197

This Rat-as-newspaper-owner series apparently angered some newspaper publishers. I know this because they refused to run some of the strips (see the commentary for the 5/3 Sunday strip). Personally, I found it rather amazing that they would block them, especially given that newspapers are normally such staunch defenders of free speech.

This strip arose out of a story I read where an editorial cartoonist was fired from his newspaper in a cost-cutting move and then unceremoniously escorted from the building. I couldn't believe they had escorted him out, and so I wrote this strip.

I did this strip at a time when newspapers really were making massive cuts to the size and content of their papers (and, unfortunately, they still are). While many editors and newspaper staffers loved it (or so I was told), some publishers did not, and they refused to run the strip in their papers. So on the Sunday that the strip ran, I got e-mails from people at certain papers telling me that *Pearls* was no longer in their paper. At first I thought I had just suffered a wave of cancellations, but then I realized the papers were just removing that day's strip due to its content.

I thought this character had some potential when I first drew him, but I got bored with him after just three strips. When I say "bored," I mean I didn't like all the work involved in drawing that bathroom.

Is it me, or does the shark look like he has grown considerably since yesterday?

This strip received a *huge* response, all of it positive. Apparently, I'm not the only person William Faulkner confused.

Eventually, these Rat-as-newspaper-owner strips angered the head of an entire newspaper chain, who began complaining to my syndicate. The newspaper chain was upset over my depiction of newspapers as a declining entity and started providing me with statistics on how newspapers were actually doing *great*, which was pretty contrary to the cuts we had all been seeing in the newspaper business over the last year or so. Moreover, the chain refused to run any strips where I was at all critical of newspapers. This resulted in some real absurdities later on when they refused to run strips that made even tangential comments about newspapers.

When I see someone with a whole bunch of bumper stickers on their car, I'm afraid to even look at them. I'm convinced they're psycho.

"Emilio" the croc is named after my best friend, Emilio. I took great joy in making him the croc with the shortest tail.

One of the best parts about doing a comic strip is the words you get to make up for various sound effects, like "Dinky Dinky Dink." While a tail-shake obviously wouldn't sound like that, it manages to convey the feeling of something small.

A more subtle commentary on my friend Emilio. This was "Knock Emilio Week" in *Pearls Before Swine*.

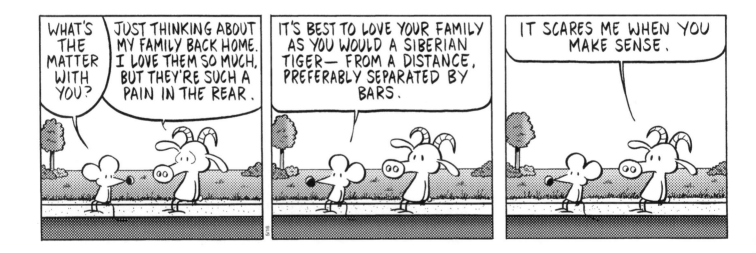

A unique strip this week in that it doesn't make fun of Emilio.

I tried to sit in a hammock once and fell out of it. This is why I don't climb mountains.

I almost didn't run this, simply because I thought it would confuse too many people. In fact, I think it's the only strip I've ever done where I've attempted to explain the joke in the space between the panels (look between the second and third panels). As it turned out, it was pretty well received.

Sadly, Pig's drawing of himself is not that different from the version I draw.

I was once bitten by a poodle in Pennsylvania. I was also bitten by an Alaskan husky in Pennsylvania. I should probably stay out of Pennsylvania.

My Yiayia Joy (my mom's mom) died when I was five. Pig's feelings are mine here.

Oh, man, this elicited all kinds of email from people explaining to me that "schadenfreude" is not "wishing ill on others," but taking pleasure from the misfortunes of others. I knew that at the time, but it didn't work for the joke. Sometimes people confuse me for the *Encyclopedia Britannica*.

I loosely modeled Rat's hat on the one Johnny Carson used when he was Carnac the Magnificent.

209

Pig's hat is a shout-out to my alma mater, the University of California.

While being interviewed by a technology writer for the *New York Times*, I casually mentioned that I had done a strip about Andy Grove. It turned out she knew him. Long story short, the original of this strip is now hanging in Andy Grove's office.

I think this is one of my favorite Danny Donkey strips. The part I like best is the stupid look of shock on the little devil's face as Danny hops the fence.

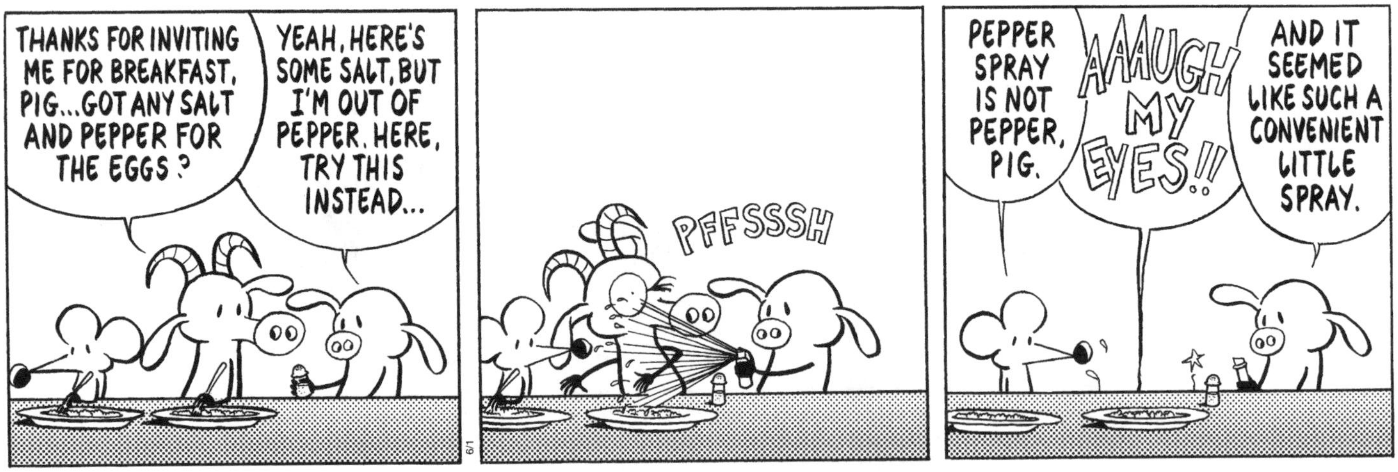
THANKS FOR INVITING ME FOR BREAKFAST, PIG...GOT ANY SALT AND PEPPER FOR THE EGGS?
YEAH, HERE'S SOME SALT, BUT I'M OUT OF PEPPER. HERE, TRY THIS INSTEAD...
PFFSSSH
PEPPER SPRAY IS NOT PEPPER, PIG.
AAAUGH MY EYES!!
AND IT SEEMED LIKE SUCH A CONVENIENT LITTLE SPRAY.

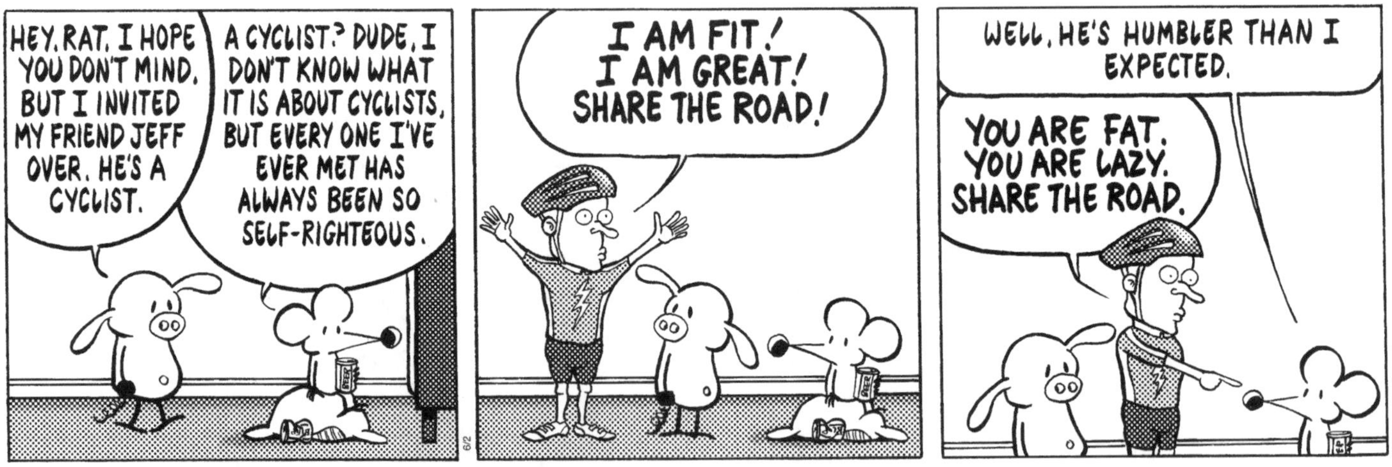
HEY, RAT. I HOPE YOU DON'T MIND, BUT I INVITED MY FRIEND JEFF OVER. HE'S A CYCLIST.
A CYCLIST? DUDE, I DON'T KNOW WHAT IT IS ABOUT CYCLISTS, BUT EVERY ONE I'VE EVER MET HAS ALWAYS BEEN SO SELF-RIGHTEOUS.
I AM FIT! I AM GREAT! SHARE THE ROAD!
WELL, HE'S HUMBLER THAN I EXPECTED.
YOU ARE FAT. YOU ARE LAZY. SHARE THE ROAD.

This was way more popular than I thought it would be, among both cyclists and people annoyed by cyclists.

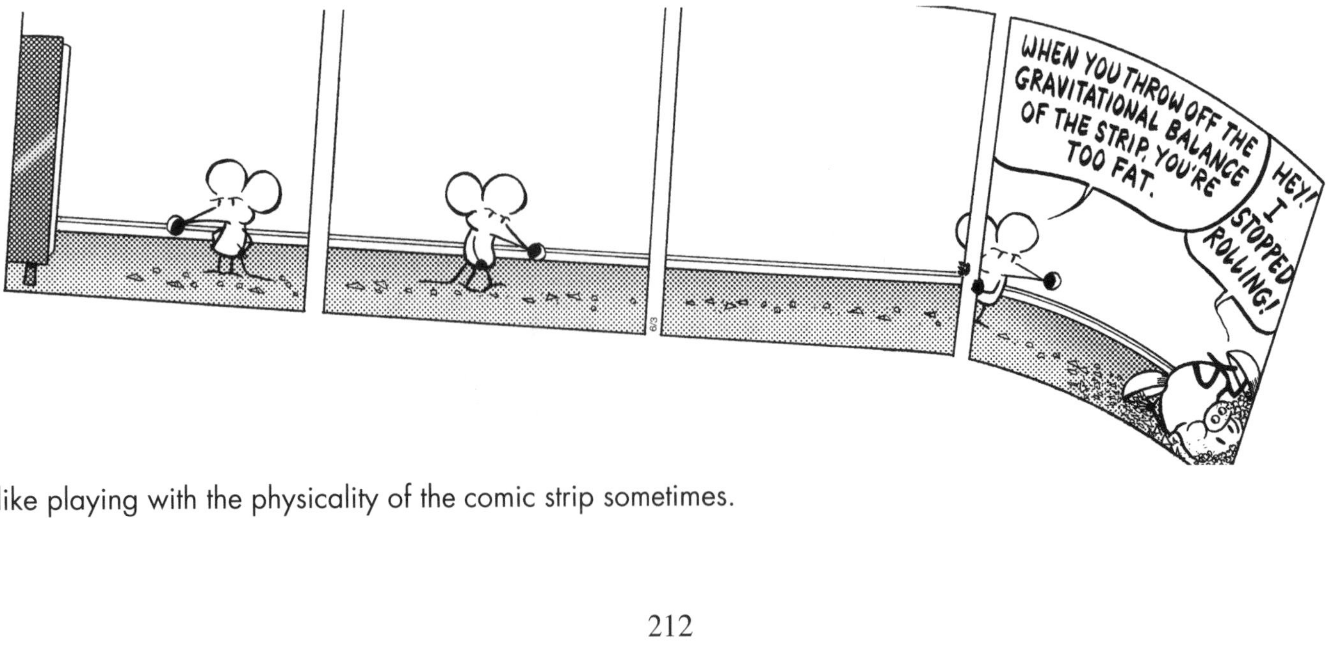
WHEN YOU THROW OFF THE GRAVITATIONAL BALANCE OF THE STRIP, YOU'RE TOO FAT.
HEY! I STOPPED ROLLING!

I like playing with the physicality of the comic strip sometimes.

This strip was the result of me driving by a café that had this sign and phonetically reading it to myself as "wifey." It turned out to be a very popular strip. It's amazing how many times the strips I spend the least time thinking up are the ones that are most popular. Maybe there's a lesson in there about overthinking humor.

All these Wii strips are straight out of my own life. I love playing the Wii with my son, but he is always moving on to new games and doesn't want to play the ones I want to play. Sometimes I have to beg and plead to get him to play with me.

I'm always in awe of the *Calvin and Hobbes* Sunday strips where there are just a number of small panels (usually of Calvin at the dinner table or something) and almost no dialogue. This was my own little humble attempt at such a strip.

I always find it interesting that we're willing to kill little things with such ease. Is it just because of their size?

I think Rat's at his best when he's insulting others.

RAT, THE BOOK EDITOR

Dear Sir,
Thank you for your manuscript, which I recently reviewed.

Had I been familiar with the literary merit of your work, I probably would not have reviewed it while my dog was on my lap.

I say this because at one point during my review, my dog took one look at your prose and died.

I LIKE TO MAKE THEM FEEL AS BAD AS POSSIBLE.

TONIGHT ON 'NATIONAL GEOGRAPHIC,' WE EXPLORE THE WORLD OF AFRICAN PREDATORS AND THEIR PREY. SO COME....

...JOIN US.

THEY DON'T MEAN IT LITERALLY, DAD.

Whoa. Ees dark een Afreeca.

Do any TVs still come with legs that are supposed to rest on the floor? Or does that only occur in my comic strip?

LOOK AT THAT OLD WOMAN IN HER CAR. SHE DRIVES SO SLOW. IF ANYTHING, YOU'D THINK OLD PEOPLE WOULD DRIVE FAST.

WHY FAST?

THEY HAVE LESS TIME LEFT.

I WISH YOU HAD LESS TIME LEFT.

THE CLOCK IS TICKING, LADY!!

I've recently learned that newspaper comic polls are dominated by older people. They appear to be the only readers who turn in their ballots. Perhaps I should stop doing strips reminding them that they're going to die soon.

A very popular pun strip, as most of the Sunday pun strips seem to be. Now if I could only draw a watermelon that doesn't look like a giant Easter egg.

On the day I drew this strip, a newspaper photographer was scheduled to take a picture of me drawing. Little did I expect that he would stay for the entire time it took me to draw the strip. Because he was right over my shoulder most of the time, I kept screwing up (even more than I normally do), and it took me forever to finish this stupid strip.

Goat's lack of skill around girls is my lack of skill around girls. Good thing I'm married, because I'd be one sad and lonely bachelor.

I have two Barbra Streisand songs on my iPod. Now tell me something embarrassing about yourself.

This was loosely based on the alleged conversation that Ernest Hemingway once had with F. Scott Fitzgerald about rich people. Fitzgerald said, "The rich are different than you and me." And Hemingway answered, "Yes, they have more money."

This was inspired by a woman who often calls my wife and leaves the world's longest messages. Of course, I probably shouldn't talk, as I've been known to call other cartoonists when they're not home just so I can sing "Ol' Man River" on their answering machine.

This was such an obvious idea for Rat that I was surprised I hadn't done it already.

Just so you know, I can only draw one type of flower. And that's the one Pig is throwing. Should I ever be asked to illustrate the *World Encyclopedia of Flowers,* this will be a big limitation.

I do *not* have any Barry Manilow songs on my iPod. And if you do, I'm here to tell you, that's a lot more embarrassing than Barbra Streisand.

My daughter has a big rock collection, and every time she shows it to me, I try to memorize the different types of rock. But because it's been a few months since we've gone through the collection, here is what I remember: Some of them are shiny.

My career will have been a success if one day I am on a subway or street corner and hear a sneeze followed by someone saying, "Chuck Norris." Please, do what you can to push this trend along.

In one of the strangest coincidences of my drawing career, this strip appeared immediately after the tragic death of pop star Michael Jackson, making it look like I had done the strip in reference to Jackson's death (which of course I hadn't; it was done many months prior). But even odder, as some readers pointed out, the "famous person" that Pig thinks up is wearing two white gloves, and Jackson's trademark was one white glove. Even odder still, in the nursery rhyme, Humpty Dumpty falls off the wall, which just so happens to be the name of one of Jackson's albums (*Off the Wall*). I'd like to be humble about all this, but clearly I'm some kind of prophet.

I have this exact same underwear. I like to wear it when I write the strip. Should there ever be a Stephan T. Pastis Museum and Research Center, I'd like this underwear to be enshrined in a glass case in the lobby.

Joyce is one of my real-life cousins. But I don't think she reads the strip, so she probably doesn't know she died.

Rat is carrying one of those Bose iPod docks, which is what I usually play my music on. I can't believe how much sound that little thing can put out.

Rat's quote is actually from Joe Pesci in one of the *Lethal Weapon* movies, but Pesci used a four-letter word, rather than the five-letter word my swear squiggles would indicate. I originally had just four swear squiggles, but it too clearly telegraphs the word Pesci used, and I knew that would create a problem for sensitive newspaper readers, all of whom seem to have nothing better to do than write their editor and complain.

Embarrassing as this is to admit, this came out of my own life. I never know what to get my wife, Staci, for her birthday, so I always have to ask her. One year, she asked for a tape measure.

In an age when fewer and fewer people read, politicians rely more and more on fear. And they'll continue to do it, because it works. That was my inspiration for this little series.

Mr. Heebie Jeebie sounds a lot like Homer Simpson here.

I have to say, I find the whole Terror Alert chart to be one of the dumbest things ever created. As far as I can see, it's just another way for politicians to exploit fear at opportune moments.

This was Guard Duck's triumphal return after being gone from the strip for a few months.

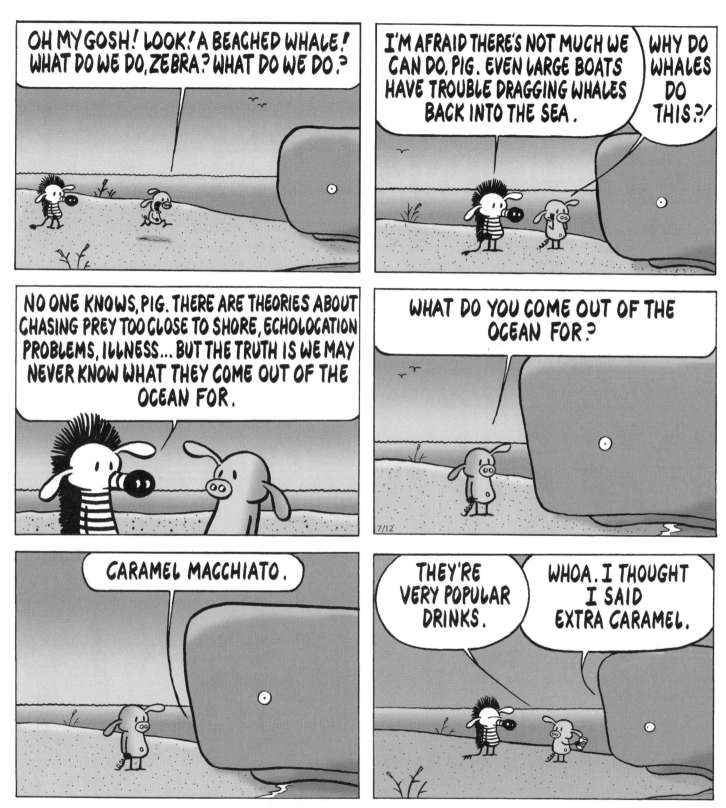

I did some field research here and asked an employee at my local Starbucks what their most popular drink was. She said caramel macchiatos. Given that the only thing I ever order from Starbucks is plain old coffee, I couldn't even tell you what a caramel macchiato is.

It's funny for me to look through this week of strips and see how different the chickens look in each strip. I was clearly learning how to draw chickens. For example, here they have googly eyes and a traditionally shaped body.

Now they just have regular dots for eyes.

Now their heads are very round, and they have wings.

Now they have long, skinny people-type necks.

By this day, I think I finally had them looking like I wanted them to look. Of course, the series was now over. So a lot of good that did me.

This arose out of real life. Someone I casually knew died suddenly in the middle of the night, and he was around my age. So I asked people who knew him better than I did all of these questions to somehow find something that differentiated him from me.

I subtly plugged two great comic strips on my mug there: Paul Gilligan's *Pooch Café* in the first panel and Richard Thompson's *Cul de Sac* in the second.

I would make fun of serial strips a lot more if I could draw their characters. This drawing of Mary Worth took me forever.

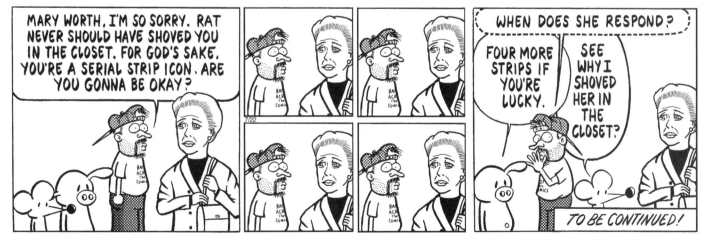

This drawing of Mary Worth took even longer. So after doing it once, I cut and pasted it five times. Had I not done that, I would still be drawing this particular strip today.

Mental note: Never draw Mary Worth again.

The female character in the first panel is Alice from *Cul de Sac*, the same strip I plugged earlier in the week. And the boy is Mark Tatulli's Liō, a character who does not talk (thus, the joke here).

Man, I was really worried about this strip, but it got no complaints at all.

Originally, this did not say "corn chips." Instead, it used the name of a very popular brand of corn chips, a name you can probably guess. But my syndicate was concerned that the company that makes those corn chips would get upset when they saw someone being strangled with one of their bags, so they asked me to change it.

There's now a message board on comics.com where people can comment on that day's *Pearls* strip, but I never read it. Reading comments about your strip online is a sure way to mess up your writing process.

This arose from my being in a café and hearing someone refer to the coffee being sold there as "bottomless." I had never heard the term before, but I knew I had to use it in the strip. It resulted in both this strip and the 8/7 strip later in the book.

This was a way more popular strip than I thought it would be.

On some days, I just get bored and want to try new things, like the warped perspective on the door here and the elaborate drawing of Hell (elaborate for me, that is). It doesn't always work, but it does break up the usual look of the strip.

Man, this one is really bizarre. Sometimes I look at certain strips and they don't even look like my work. I sit back and think, "Who wrote that one?"

This one took me by complete surprise. It generated all sorts of complaints from people vociferously defending the tenure system and telling me how hard professors have it. And the ridiculous thing was that I didn't care one iota about the tenure system. I just thought it would be funny to misconstrue the idea of tenure to the point that it enabled a person to do anything they wanted in life, like blowing up buildings. And yet I had somehow walked into the middle of an issue that a lot of uptight people felt very strongly about.

Let it be known that I have a full head of hair.

Online comic polls are just invitations to cheat. And yet some editors continue to use them without taking any safeguards to ensure they are fair and honest. How would they like their jobs determined by a rigged poll?

When my dad comes to stay at our house, I always have to explain the remote controls to him. He nods his head like he's understanding what I'm saying, but I know he's just thinking, "Forget it. I won't even turn the $*%# thing on."

This was the other "bottomless" coffee joke, although this one was a bit more graphic.

The fat "Backstreet Boy" I had in mind was actually a member of "'N Sync," but "'N Sync" is an odd name that might cause you to have to read it twice. So I just said "Backstreet Boy" instead. I never want to include a word in the middle of a joke that can potentially distract people from the joke.

This strip created an utterly ridiculous situation. An editor at a large midwestern newspaper thought he saw the F-word in the second panel. Without contacting me to ask if it was really there, he contacted a local TV station, and that night the TV news did a piece on me saying that I had inserted the F-word into my comic. They even went so far as to blur out the offending panel. When I found out, I called the editor myself and told him the word was not there. The editor swore that it *was* there, in the middle of the panel, just above the words "been living." The best I can figure out is that when the newspaper condensed the strip vertically (as some newspapers do), the word "#rock" melded with the words above it to form the F-word. But it was not put there by me.

I believe I wrote these at the time that everyone was freaking out about swine flu.

I just noticed that Pig's mask went from white yesterday to dark today. I can't explain that.

I knew at the time that everyone was complaining about the 8/2 strip that this next strip was still upcoming. Naturally, it triggered a whole new round of angry e-mails from people who desperately needed to get a life.

I see that instead of writing "beer" on the cans as I normally do, I wrote "brewski." If you noticed that on your own, give yourself one *Pearls* point.

Larry's photo is a lot like my own grade school photos, when I had both glasses and braces. But later I blossomed into a beautiful man.

Regarding the comment below that last strip, I don't *really* think I'm a beautiful man.

Regarding the comment about the comment below that last strip, I sort of do.

I will end now before I say anything else stupid. I've done enough damage to my reputation with these unfiltered comments. Goodbye until the next treasury.

Portrait of a Cartoonist as a Young Man

Me and my Yiayia Joy (my grandma), circa 1970.

When I was a kid reading Gary Larson's *The Far Side*® or Bill Watterson's *Calvin and Hobbes*, I always wanted to know what Gary Larson or Bill Watterson looked like. Was there a resemblance between Larson and the big-nosed, four-eyed people he drew? Did Bill Watterson look like a grown-up Calvin, or did he look like Calvin's father? Nowadays, in the age of the Internet, knowing what an idiot like me looks like is as easy as Googling "Stephan Pastis." But I didn't just spring forth an idiot. I matured into one. So in the interest of showing how a little ugly duckling like me flowered into the big ugly duck I am today, I present this brief photographic tour of my life.

For those who wonder why beer drinking plays such a prominent role in *Pearls,* look no further than my first fort, the padded Coors box.

Me as a toddler scoping the babes in Newport Beach, California. Every time I'd come close to getting a phone number, my mom would ruin it by trying to dress me.

Here I am with my sisters, Penny and Parisa, neither of whom was sophisticated enough to appreciate the witty one-liner I've just gotten off.

Stephan the Little League slugger. It wasn't until I went 0-for-the-entire-season at the plate that I realized I needed glasses.

Skinny, four-eyed, but phenomenally strong.

There is dressing your kid funny, and then there is *dressing your kid funny*. Clearly the same mom who ruined my chance with the beach babes was going to kill any chance I had of meeting girls in our nation's capital.

Me with my dad on the day of my junior high graduation in 1982. Thankfully, in the years to come, I would learn how to button my sportcoat.

Me intoxicated for the first time in my life, in the summer of 1986. I was so excited to be drunk that I ran to the stereo and listened to "The End" by the Doors to see if it sounded any different. Sadly, it sounded pretty much the same.

Me on the day of my high school graduation with the same two sisters who failed to laugh at my sophisticated toddler humor a few pages ago.

At college in my favorite piece of clothing I have ever owned: my beloved leather jacket. I cannot explain the tight jeans.

Ahhh, college.

There is no significance to this photo of me in Laughlin, Nevada. I just think I look good.

Me making Staci laugh on our wedding day. Finally, someone who finds me funny.

Me conceiving of the comic strip *Pearls Before Swine* while sitting in front of the Parthenon in Greece. Okay, fine, I don't know what I was thinking about, but it sounds good.

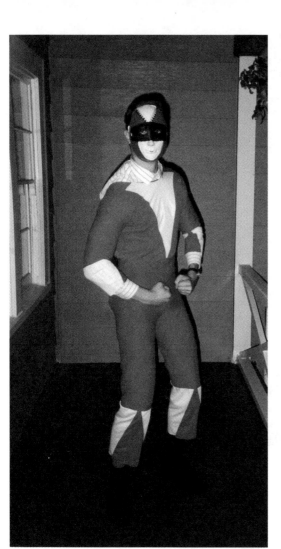

The Power Rangers suit I wore one day to my law firm. Photographic evidence of why I was not suited to be a lawyer.

This is the basement of our former house in Albany, California. It is where I first drew *Pearls Before Swine*. One day I went downstairs to draw and discovered my office had become a lake (due to a sump pump that had failed under the basement floor). It made drawing difficult.

Me relaxing in our backyard (or at Hearst Castle). I get them confused.

Me with my fellow cartoonists on our USO tour of Baghdad, Iraq, in November 2009. Back row (left to right): Me, Mike Ramirez, Jeff Keane, Jeff Bacon, Rick Kirkman, Tom Richmond. Front row (left to right): Garry Trudeau, Mike Peters, Chip Bok.